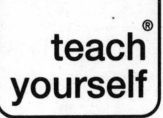

teach yourself

single parenting

D1531832

single parenting
suzie hayman

Launched in 1938, the **teach yourself** series grew rapidly in response to the world's wartime needs. Loved and trusted by over 50 million readers, the series has continued to respond to society's changing interests and passions and now, 70 years on, includes over 500 titles, from Arabic and Beekeeping to Yoga and Zulu. What would you like to learn?

be where you want to be with **teach yourself**

For UK order enquiries: please contact Bookpoint Ltd, 130 Milton Park, Abingdon, Oxon, OX14 4SB. Telephone: +44 (0) 1235 827720. Fax: +44 (0) 1235 400454. Lines are open 09.00–17.00, Monday to Saturday, with a 24-hour message answering service. Details about our titles and how to order are available at www.teachyourself.co.uk

For USA order enquiries: please contact McGraw-Hill Customer Services, PO Box 545, Blacklick, OH 43004-0545, USA. Telephone: 1-800-722-4726. Fax: 1-614-755-5645.

For Canada order enquiries: please contact McGraw-Hill Ryerson Ltd, 300 Water St, Whitby, Ontario, L1N 9B6, Canada. Telephone: 905 430 5000. Fax: 905 430 5020.

Long renowned as the authoritative source for self-guided learning – with more than 50 million copies sold worldwide – the **teach yourself** series includes over 500 titles in the fields of languages, crafts, hobbies, business, computing and education.

British Library Cataloguing in Publication Data: a catalogue record for this title is available from the British Library.

Library of Congress Catalog Card Number: on file.

First published in UK 2008 by Hodder Education, part of Hachette Livre UK, 338 Euston Road, London, NW1 3BH.

First published in US 2008 by The McGraw-Hill Companies, Inc.

This edition published 2008.

The **teach yourself** name is a registered trade mark of Hodder Headline.

Typeset by Transet Limited, Coventry, England.
Printed in Great Britain for Hodder Education, part of Hachette Livre UK, 338 Euston Road, London, NW1 3BH, by Cox & Wyman Ltd, Reading, Berkshire.

The publisher has used its best endeavours to ensure that the URLs for external websites referred to in this book are correct and active at the time of going to press. However, the publisher and the author have no responsibility for the websites and can make no guarantee that a site will remain live or that the content will remain relevant, decent or appropriate.

Hachette Livre UK's policy is to use papers that are natural, renewable and recyclable products and made from wood grown in sustainable forests. The logging and manufacturing processes are expected to conform to the environmental regulations of the country of origin.

Impression number   10 9 8 7 6 5 4 3 2 1
Year   2012 2011 2010 2009 2008

contents

acknowledgements

This book is, with thanks, for all the single parents who showed me that the myths are such a lot of rubbish – it may be hard, but so is any sort of parenting. So here's to love, fun and togetherness – the realities of single parenting.

And it's with enormous thanks to the best editor in the world, Victoria Roddam. Wow, the patience of the woman! Thank you so much for being tolerant, long suffering and enabling!

introduction

A few facts

If you are raising children on your own you may feel isolated and under pressure, but you aren't alone. There are 1.8 million lone parents with 3 million children in the UK, and almost 10 million lone parents in the USA, so you no longer have reason to feel different or unusual. Families of all shapes and sizes are becoming more common. You are three times more likely to live in a one-parent household now than you were in 1972 and, by 2010, the 'traditional' family of husband and wife with two plus children will no longer be the norm.

Overturning the stereotypes

Clearly the 'bad press' that single parents attract makes your life more difficult. Most single parent families – nine out of ten – are headed by mothers. Newspapers and magazines seem to demonize women who become single parents, although everyone seems to be sympathetic and supportive when it's a single dad. The reasons for you being on your own are endlessly (and mostly inaccurately) rehashed, with judgements made and criticism levelled.

Some of the stereotypes of single parents, apart from the idea they are all women, seem to be that they are young, unmarried, work-shy and 'don't-care' benefit scroungers. Behind the statistics are real people, and the real stories show a very different picture. For a start, before they became lone parents almost half of single mothers were married, in their first and only partnership. It's true that the figure for cohabiting couples is going up in the UK, as it is across Europe and the USA. In the UK 20 years ago, 10 per cent of births were to unmarried couples. Today it is nearer 30 per cent. And statistics seem to suggest that unmarried relationships are more fragile than married ones. But that still does not justify the myth that all lone parents begin parenthood lightly or on shaky foundations. The vast majority have either married only once or lived in only one relationship, or else been married once and lived with one other person.

Confounding another myth is the fact that the peak age for single mothers is actually early 30s and for fathers early 40s. The ages of single parents may range from teenage to late 50s but the majority of them are over 25. That seems to contradict the image that single mums are young women who have babies to leave home and get themselves a council house. And far from being work shy, 55 per cent of lone parents are in work – a high figure when you factor in the enormous hurdles that a parent on their own must overcome to manage a home, children and a job.

How this book will help

Although many of the stereotypes are unfounded, it is true that being a single parent is hardly the easiest situation to be in. However, it doesn't have to be any harder to be in a single parent family than in a two parent family and that's what this book is all about – taking some of the hard work out so you can put the fun back in. If you're a single parent you may have a number of concerns, which this book hopes to address. The top ten issues for single parents are likely to be:

- **Money** – *see Chapters 07 and 08*
- **Regrets and concerns about becoming a single parent** – *see Chapter 01*
- **Feelings of guilt and failure** – *see Chapter 02*
- **Your child's emotional well-being** – *see Chapter 03*
- **Isolation and loneliness** – *see Chapters 04 and 09*
- **Contact with the child's other parent** – *see Chapters 04 and 08*
- **Worries about parenting skills** – *see Chapter 05*
- **Childcare** – *see Chapter 07*
- **Your own and your child's future** – *see Chapter 06*
- **New relationships, making them and keeping them** – *see Chapter 10.*

Barbara Frum 416-395-5440

Toronto Public Library

User ID: 2 ********** 1926

Date Format: DD/MM/YYYY

Number of Items: 1

Item ID:37131094397478
Title:Single parenting
Date due:22/02/2018

Telephone Renewal# 416-395-5505
www.torontopubliclibrary.ca
Thursday, February 1, 2018 6:04 PM

. . .

This book will cover all of this and more – it is your guide to being a single parent. Being a parent in any type of family is never easy. It's hard work but it's also fun, exciting and joyful. When something has happened to your family that has derailed it from the path you might have expected, you can easily lose sight of the good parts. Most of us imagine having children will be something we'll do with a partner – someone who loves and supports us, and loves and supports our children. If we find ourselves with a family on our own, it's usually because of some form of loss. You might have lost your partner because they died or your relationship died. Maybe a relationship you had expected to develop came to a sudden and premature end, either because the other person let you down or because you realized they were not the person you thought they were. Or perhaps you came to a point in your life when time ran out. You waited long enough for the right partner or the right relationship and decided if you didn't have children on your own, you'd never have children at all.

When you feel alone you may get the idea that there's little help available, or that everyone is looking down on you for being in your situation and expecting you to fail. Instead of feeling happy about your family and confident about your ability to be a parent, you may feel scared, lost and alone. That's where **Teach Yourself Single Parenting** comes in!

This book is about looking forward and helping you to take charge of your life, your family and your choices, whether you are a single mum or a single dad, whatever your age and income. The single parent life may seem overwhelming. The good news is that you have a lot more going for you than you might think. This book will arm you with the facts and lots of ideas of what to do, who to ask and where to go. But the important thing is that, with a bit of help, *you* can do most of it for yourself. You can:

- take pleasure in your family and your children
- understand the skills needed to be a parent and value your own competence
- feel confident and worthwhile, as a parent and as an individual
- foster your own support networks and see their value
- develop communication and other skills, both for your family and outside the home
- recognize that all parents need help from time to time and see asking for support as a sign of strength rather than weakness.

Above all, you'll realize that all parents worry about many of these issues – money, isolation, parenting skills, your child's well-being. Parenting is a hard job whoever you are and whatever your situation. Once you have made use of **Teach Yourself Single Parenting,** you'll have the confidence to know that you are the expert you need to manage your family the way you would like.

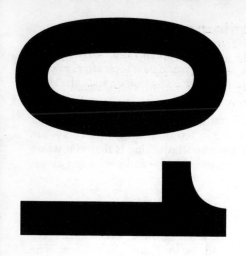

01

in the beginning

In this chapter you will learn:
- who becomes a single parent
- about the myths and misapprehensions surrounding single parents
- how to come to terms with your new state
- to understand the emotions you might go through
- how to use these emotions to your advantage
- how and when to tell the children and anyone else involved.

Becoming a single parent

You're on your own, with a child or children. And you're in good company. Around 1.8 million women and men look after children on their own in the UK today, almost 10 million do so in the USA.

You're probably a mother, because most lone parents are mothers, but you may be a father on your own. An increasing number of dads – around one in ten of all single parents – are now lone parents too. But the important thing is that you won't be a stereotype, you will be an individual – and you're not alone.

Who becomes a single parent?

Single parents come from every background, every age, every learning and earning level and all jobs and professions. The single parents that hit the headlines and thus form many people's opinions about what it means to be a lone parent are teenagers. But even then, the stereotype is usually imprecise. Many teenage mums have been married, are living in homes of their own, are in jobs or studying for qualifications, and are determined not to let their lone state change their prospects.

Lone mothers do not, on the whole, become such because they were single when they fell pregnant. Neither is the impression that most single parents drift from relationship to relationship in any way accurate. The vast majority of lone mothers have either married only once to their first serious partner, or lived in only one relationship, or else been married once and lived with one other person. Bereavement and widowhood play less of a part in making single parents than they used to, only because more people get divorced now. But that too is a significant section of lone parents.

Being a single parent isn't something that only happens to young people either. Most single parents take up the reins on their own some way into what they might have expected to be a settled and stable relationship, in their early 30s or 40s.

The shock

Whether it was divorce, separation, bereavement or abandonment that left you on your own, it may well have been a shock. In some cases a realization that the relationship is going to end slowly dawns. With other single parents, it comes as a complete surprise – little warning, no time to plan. You may be where you are now because of a death – the death of your partner or the death of your relationship together. It might have been a slow process, with a gradual illness that made you realize you were soon going to have to manage on your own or a long period of bitter arguments. Or perhaps you thought you had an understanding with your partner and either the pregnancy or some other trigger has resulted in them making it clear that they never intended, or no longer intend, to be by your side. In any case, when an ending looms into sight most of us stick our heads in the sand. You might have made some practical plans but the chances are you put off anything that would have prepared you emotionally for being on your own.

The ending may have come suddenly, with an accident or sudden illness or the horrible discovery that your partner has betrayed you or no longer loves you, or that you no longer love them, resulting in an immediate break-up. One day they were there and the next, gone.

From the postbag

My husband walked out on me two months ago and I feel such a fool. I thought we had the perfect marriage – two lovely children, a nice house. OK, we didn't spend as much time as I'd like together and we had our arguments but I was just shattered to learn he'd been having an affair for over a year. He didn't go to stay with her – he says it's over but he's not coming back. I thought at first he'd come to his senses but now he's buying a flat so I think he means it. I feel as if the whole marriage – our children, our life together – was a lie and I don't know how to go on.

It feels painful now and will always be a source of regret and disappointment, but eventually you'll be able to look back on the good bits of your marriage and appreciate that they still exist and are still real. The sad ending doesn't take away the happy beginning, nor what came out of you relationship – years of trust and two lovely children that both of you still love. It might help to ask if he'd go to counselling with you, not to put the marriage back together but to enable you to part with a degree of dignity and closure – he owes you that. Once you can understand why he did what he did and can feel he has heard your anger and disillusionment you may be able to move on. You may feel you can never trust him again as a partner but can do so as a co-parent, and that you will be able to trust someone else again. Good luck!

Is it always something you regret?

Becoming a single parent can be a very positive beginning rather than a painful end. With the pain and grief can often come a sense of release. If your lone parent state is the result of a break-up, both you and your children may heave a deep sigh of relief, as the conflict and arguments, the tension and sometimes the violence stop. With the other person gone, perhaps you and your family can breathe easily again. Even after an illness and death, there may be some sense of relief that now the waiting, the suspense and the suffering is over.

Whichever it was, in the immediate aftermath of the departure of the other parent, you need to come to terms with what has happened and what you are now facing. You may be reading this some time after the actual split – if you didn't come to terms with what happened then you may need to now. Coming to terms with the situation is your chance to take control and make this a positive situation even if at the moment you don't feel it is.

How to come to terms with becoming a single parent

Coming to terms with a new situation, and one that may be very different from the one you might have envisaged, is a process. You can't expect it to happen overnight. Indeed, it often takes far longer than that. The process begins with the emotional fallout from the split. When anything happens that brings you up short – a death, a relationship break-up, the realization that what you thought was going on between you was very different from your partner's views – people tend to go through a progression of reactions and emotions.

Shock

For most people the first reaction is shock. You may feel numb, dazed and confused. You may be surprised at how little pain or anguish you feel, and find yourself operating on automatic, going through the motions and getting by. Shock is actually a survival mechanism and your lack of sensation is the point – it's how you cope. It doesn't mean you won't feel the pain of what has happened eventually and it doesn't mean you are abnormal or unfeeling. Shock helps you manage in the immediate aftermath, when a cool head may be needed to manage the urgent arrangements that you'll have to make to deal with being left on your own.

Denial

At some point a lot of people go into denial. When given bad news, most of us begin to question it pretty soon. Are we certain it happened? Surely there must have been a mistake. Just you wait and see, it will all turn out to have been a slip-up and everything will go back to the way it was before. If your partner has died you may become convinced the hospital or doctor made a blunder and will be in touch to say they're actually getting better. If your partner has left, or you've left them, you may convince yourself the arguments weren't as bad as all that and you'll soon be able to make up and begin again.

Anger

After denial usually comes anger. You may be furious at the person who has gone – even if their leaving was not their choice. It's absolutely normal to be enraged at someone who has died, as odd and unfair as it may seem. After all, they left you. They abandoned you. Of course you feel angry. Feelings aren't fair or logical – feelings are feelings, the outpourings of our primitive selves and they don't pay any attention to reason or sense. But, of course, you may have every reason to be angry, if you've been let down, cheated and abandoned. The problem with anger is that it frequently doesn't stay in bounds. Instead of being directed at the person who initiated and perhaps deserves our rage we often spray it around at other people in the vicinity. Perhaps we discharge our anger on those who have not left us – children, friends and parents. And sooner or later we also often direct it onto ourselves. We may feel unable to stop, because the anger has to go somewhere and the person we're really angry at isn't around to bear the brunt.

Guilt

Guilt is another common reaction. We may feel responsible for what has happened, even if we know the situation was nobody's fault, or clearly the responsibility of another person. We may endlessly go over and over what happened, asking ourselves whether if we'd done something differently that it may have ended better, or not ended at all. Children are particularly prone to assuming guilt and blaming themselves, becoming convinced that if they'd been 'good' or not been so badly behaved that the outcome would have been different.

Depression

Single parents may be at risk of another of the reactions to sudden or problematical change: depression. Depression isn't just sadness, it's a crippling condition that saps the life out of you. If you're depressed, you're likely to find simple day-to-day tasks too much to contemplate. You may feel exhausted and too apathetic even to get up in the morning, let alone have the energy or will to focus on anything else. If you're depressed you may feel a prop such as drink or drugs may help you get through the day, or at least help you unwind when you have dragged yourself around. As with all the other reactions to a change in your circumstances, you may well not respond this way but if you do, it can be dealt with and you can get help. Read on, because we'll be dealing with all the ways you can manage these feelings later in this chapter.

Bargaining

After a loss people often go through a stage of bargaining, with themselves and fate. You may find yourself promising 'If I do this, maybe my partner will come back' or 'If I do that, maybe it will all go away'.

Acceptance

Eventually, you come to acceptance. You know it happened, it hurt and maybe you're still angry and upset and would love it to be as it was before. But you're looking forward and are prepared to deal with what you have rather than what you wish or fantasize you should have. *You have come to terms with what happened.*

Going through the stages of the process

The stages of shock, denial, anger, guilt, depression, bargaining and finally acceptance are common but entirely individual. Each person may go through all of them or some of them, and in this order or another. The progress though them may take some months or even years. Frequently people double back, getting over denial or guilt or anger to suddenly have it come back with full force, or diminished strength but, nonetheless, effect.

With the entire process, the best way of dealing with it is to recognize what is happening and to allow the gradual unfolding of this natural progression. Each stage can help you get though the difficult early days. It is best to acknowledge what is happening and understand the normality of what may initially seem to be conflicting and confusing reactions. Some of them are potentially far from helpful so by understanding and working with them you can help yourself get you through this period.

How to make shock work for you

Shock is a cushioning response to shield you from the full force of your unhappy emotions in the early stages. If you were to experience the full force of your feelings you would be overwhelmed and probably unable to function at a time when you may have work to do. To help you make plans, your feelings shut down and are held at arm's length for several days, if not weeks. Don't feel that this reaction shows you are unfeeling or that you'll never react emotionally to what has happened. Sooner or later you will unfreeze. Until you do, use this respite to get started on all those things you have to do – talking the situation through with your children, telling those who have to know, making practical arrangements for being on your own. Get set up because when the emotions come back you may need some time to rage, scream, weep into your pillow and be fragile and incompetent for a time. Do explain this to your children, however, or they may feel confused, and find it hard to confide in you how they are feeling.

How to make denial work for you

Denial can be a dangerous mindset to get into. If your partner is no longer by your side, you may have very good reasons not to want to believe that; but do you have good reason to think they might come back? People in relationships that do them no good often sweep under the carpet the recognition of how much it harms them. They may accept lies and deception, infidelity and inconstancy, as long as the partner stays with them.

Being in denial can mean you accept blame for what happened when it may have been a shared responsibility or indeed the other person's actions. In trying to make everything good again you would have to compromise your own well-being and go against the instincts telling you that you are being harmed.

Denying that something has happened can hold you up from dealing with the inevitable. As long as you go on insisting it was all a mistake and the situation will go back to how it was before, you can't move on and deal with it. This can have devastating effects on children, themselves unable to understand what has gone on and relying on you for an explanation. If you keep insisting their other parent hasn't gone or will return, they cannot begin to cope with their own feelings and reactions or to learn how to manage with the new situation.

Denial is understandable but it is best used as a challenge. If you find yourself refusing to believe, sit down with someone you trust – a friend, a relative or a counsellor – and ask yourself:

- What has happened?
- What would I like to believe is going to happen?
- Why do I think this?
- Is this a realistic belief?

Exploring the feelings and the reality will help you put denial behind you and face up to what you are going to do to manage the new situation.

How to avoid the quick fix

Ask your friend or relative to help you by listening and supporting you in finding your own solution. Often, what happens when you go for help is that people don't really listen and try to come up with the quick fix. They may make light of your fears and be dismissive of them, or they may tell you that you should be able to cope, or they may try to persuade you to do what they think they would do in such a situation.

Active listening would help. Active listening means that the person you're speaking to focuses on your words. They let you know they are hearing you and encourage you to keep talking by saying 'Uh-huh' or 'Um' or nodding and making eye contact, all to make you know they are paying attention to what you are saying. They make no comments, no interruptions, no questions – nothing to stop your flow; they simply let you know you are being heard.

But what you really need is someone who will help you with **reflective listening**. Reflective listening means that your listener mirrors back what you say to them. They can use your words or their own words. Reflective listening isn't just parroting, it's rephrasing and checking. They don't have to get it entirely right first time, every time – you can correct them and enlarge on what you are saying. The checking out and rephrasing helps you hear back what you are saying and, in correcting or agreeing with them, you clarify your points for yourself. Reflective listening allows you to put your thoughts in order and hear them yourself by trying to clearly explain yourself to someone else. Useful phrases for your listener to use in mirrored speech may be 'It sounds as if you're saying ...', 'I imagine you're feeling ...', 'It seems to me that what you're saying is ...', 'What I hear you saying is...'

How to make anger work for you

Anger is a very common reaction to the loss of a partner and finding yourself as a single parent. Mostly, the person you're angry with is the partner who has left you like this. Or you can feel anger towards people you want to think might have had a hand in what happened – a parent, friend or maybe the lover of your ex. The fury you may feel towards your partner can linger, often blocking any hope of reasonable discussion with them or about them when it comes to making plans about your family and your future. Your anger can also prevent you from having any positive thoughts about them, or happy memories. Not only is your future with them snatched away but so too is your past.

Often the anger comes out at other people. Since the person you're angry with isn't there to hear it or take the brunt of it, other people stand in. You may find yourself raging at your children, relatives or friends, or people in authority or organizations who irritate you, fail to help you or get in your way. You may have entirely good reasons to be annoyed with any of these people. Your anger, however, may be over the top because in fact it's the anger that belongs to your ex-partner that you are dumping in their laps.

Just as destructive is a tendency to turn anger on yourself. You may do this in open ways – blaming yourself, running yourself down. Or you may do it by acting self-destructively – drinking, smoking, gaining weight and generally not looking after yourself. Some of these actions you may present to yourself as actually being ways of treating yourself – the extra drink, cigarette, cream cake. If the result is actually harmful the reality is that you know, deep down, that it's self-destructive and that's really why you're doing it.

How do you deal with anger?

We all have anger and the first step is to accept and acknowledge that it's a natural emotion. We often shy away from facing up to negative emotions because we fear that having them is somehow wrong. When we experience jealousy, anger, misery and so on, we often feel quite guilty about feeling that way. We might have been told when young that we're 'bad' when we do. So we avoid exploring the emotion, or try to blame it on someone else. This is when we claim 'You made me...', or say 'Look what you did'. We try to persuade ourselves that the other person deserves our anger because they are bad. Or, just as often, we punish ourselves for feeling that way because we feel that having these negative emotions proves that we're bad.

What is 'dirty anger'?

This destructive use of anger is dirty anger. Dirty anger is when you let anger spill out in uncontrolled and hurtful actions or words. It harms you as well as everyone around you. Dirty anger is when you:

- run people down, shout or hit out
- 'kick the cat' – pick on someone or something when actually it's someone or something else that has upset you
- rake over past grievances.

Dirty anger does us and our children no good at all. It makes them defensive, harms our relationship with them and damages their self-esteem. It leaves us ashamed and guilty and doesn't get the result we want. Dirty anger in a single family may result in your sounding off against the person who has let you down and you may be right to do so. Except, being the children's other parent, this can cause them extreme distress. Children often get drawn into dirty anger, blaming and shouting at the parent with whom they live instead of the parent they're really angry with, the one who has left.

Dealing with anger begins by accepting that feelings are just feelings and we can't help having them. Emotions such as anger, misery and jealousy are as natural and common as feelings such as sympathy, love and satisfaction. You deal with them by accepting it's okay to feel these things. But at the same time, you fully embrace the fact that while you cannot help your feelings you most certainly can help what you do about them. You can feel furious about the situation – and say so. You can feel angry at your ex-partner – and say so in some circumstances and to some people. You should recognize who you're really angry with or what you're angry about and not let your anger become directed at the people around you or yourself.

Understanding anger

Anger becomes destructive and runs away with us when we don't understand why and when we feel it. Anger seldom comes out of the blue – it builds up. If you could recognize when you are getting angry, what makes it happen or worsen, or what could damp it down, you might be able to get it under control. Ask yourself the following questions:

What makes you angry?

Thinking about what someone does or has done? Is it worse when you think about it, or when you see or have to interact with them? Is it their actions, or is it the way something in the situation triggers emotions – of helplessness, pain, fear? Can you remember feeling like that at any other time in your life? Could your anger be about something in your past instead of or as much as what is going on now?

How would others recognize you are angry?

Do you go pale or red, ball up your fists, grit your teeth, go silent, start pacing around?

What are the first signs you notice in yourself?

Do you find yourself having difficulty breathing or getting your words out? Do you feel panicky, frightened or confused?

What makes your anger increase?

Is there something you do yourself that makes it worse, or does being ignored or made the centre of attention drive you further into a rage?

What makes your anger decrease?

Do you feel calmer if someone sits down and talks with you, or if you're left alone?

What do you do with your angry feelings?

Do you shout, hit out or run away? Do you try to bury the feelings and pretend you're okay, go silent or keep on bringing it up? Do you pick fights with other people or shout at the family? Do you go and do the washing up, go for a drink or a walk?

Write down your answers and look at them. Does anything you've written give you ideas that you can use to come up with a plan for how to deal with your anger next time it arises? If you can understand why it happens, can you change the triggers that set off the anger? If you can see the warning signs, can you talk about it? If you know what makes it worse, or makes it better, can you use this knowledge to abate it? If you can find a helpful way of getting rid of the anger, can you make use of it?

Are there ways of expressing anger safely?

There is nothing wrong with anger, only with how we may express and show it. Anger needs to be recognized, accepted and expressed. The destructive nature of your anger may make you fear for yourself and for those with whom you are angry. It may feel frightening and this may cause you to want to hide it. The problem with unexpressed anger is that it will come out, often in less helpful ways. Violence or destructive conflict and circular, continuing arguments in families tend to be about rage that isn't being handled in a constructive way by the person experiencing the anger. Sometimes that fury has its roots in the past, and is triggered by something that happens in the present and reminds the person of their earlier feelings of helplessness, loss or fear. The fury may become all the more violent because they are trying to keep the feelings and the anger under wraps. Or it may show itself in more subtle ways such as poor self-esteem, depression or ill health. This is why it is useful to have ways of expressing your anger safely. Here are some ideas – add your own:

Physical ways of expressing anger

- Ripping up newspapers or old phone books.
- Throwing, kicking or punching soft objects such as pillows, cushions or soft toys.
- Screaming loudly – somewhere deserted such as in the middle of a park, field or under a railway bridge when the train is going over or near a busy motorway.
- Shouting, jumping up and down or rolling around on a sofa or bed.
- Doing a household job with passion – scrub a floor, dig the garden, polish windows and do it really vigorously.
- Exercising – walk briskly, run, cycle, swim, go to the gym or a keep fit class.
- Throwing things at a target – throw stones at a post in the garden or soft toys at something indoors. Pretend the target is the person or thing you're angry with.

Non-physical ways of expressing anger

- Painting your feelings. Get lots of paper, lots of colours and lots of room and splash, slash and clash your emotions out in the open.
- Writing a letter. Put exactly what you are feeling down in words. Don't send it to the person with whom you are angry – the point of this is to get it out of yourself and get rid of it. When you are satisfied you've put it all down, burn it or rip it to shreds and let it go.
- Pretending the person you are angry with is sitting in front of you and tell them what you think of them.

When you've got the anger out of you, take a deep breath and think of some positive, creative things you can do to change the situation; or accept that it's something you'll have to learn to let pass you by.

How to make guilt work for you

Most of us, when something dreadful happens, have an awful, sinking feeling that it's our fault. Maybe we did or said something that led to the event. Or maybe we didn't do enough to stop it occurring. Or, worst of all, perhaps just being us was enough to make this inevitable. We may tell ourselves off, run ourselves down and beat ourselves up over the whole situation, totally convinced that we were the ones to cause it. Children are most prone to doing this, probably because kids tend to think they are at the centre of the universe and that everything revolves around them. If you feel your rages are so dangerous and powerful that they might kill your parents and lay waste to the surrounding area – as small children do! – then it stands to reason if your world falls apart with your parents separating that you must be to blame. And even when we grow up and learn better, most of us still harbour that still, small voice that says 'It's all your fault'.

In the early days of being a single parent and later too, you may find yourself wondering over and over whether you did something to deserve and trigger your situation and whether you could have done anything different to have avoided it.

To make guilt work for you, you need to separate circular, futile blame-setting from something that could be useful – an exploration of how you manage relationships and how you might manage better in future.

Any argument, whether it's with someone else or yourself, becomes pointless when all you do is endlessly rehash what *might* have happened or who *might* have done what, and never move on. The trick is to challenge your guilt and make it a spur to constructive action.

Who is to blame is unimportant. Who may be responsible could be useful to recognize. If you contributed to the situation that led to you being a single parent because you found it hard to make and keep relationships, or because you tend to choose partners who let you down, then making changes could help you for the future. But dwelling on the past does not and cannot help.

Ask yourself 'What have I lost?'

Look at what was good about the situation before you became a single parent. Your relationship? A carefree life? Face up to the fact that you've lost something and feel awful about it. Mourn: cry, scream, hit pillows, tear up tissues, throw china, **and then get over it**. Once you feel you're done with mourning, take a deep breath, dry the tears and get ready to move on.

Ask yourself 'What have I gained?'

The best way to banish guilt is to recognize what you might have gained by the change in circumstances. Once you set your mind to it, you may find a surprising list of positive benefits. Sit down with paper and pen and list them. You might come up with:

• having the right to make your own choices
• an end to quarrels
• peace and quiet
• the return of self-confidence
• happier, more secure kids.

Writing down the positives about your new situation will help you to recognize that all is not lost and that you don't need to feel guilty.

Ask yourself 'What was good about my past relationship?'

It is not helpful to make the missing person a monster or the sole author of your woes, for many reasons which we'll cover later. You might think reframing the past in totally negative terms may help you cope with its loss. In fact, it's more helpful to hold onto what was good about it. List what was good and what you'll miss about your previous situation. You might write:

• having someone to lean on
• being loved
• having fun with your partner
• the good aspects of your relationship, and your ex
• sharing problems
• some financial certainty.

What was good will be your guide for your future. Because the truth is that while you might have felt that all the good stuff only came about while with or because of your partner, you can look after yourself and make as many good things happen for yourself.

Ask yourself 'How could I do better?'

The final challenge to your guilt is to look at what lessons it may have for you. You may need to recognize that some of the choices and decisions you made might have been better. Think about the partner you chose, the relationship you had and the arguments you were involved in. Are you in a pattern that may be unfortunate or unhelpful, or downright destructive? Ask yourself:

- What sort of partners do I tend to pick?
- What sort of relationships do I tend to find myself in?
- What attracts me to my partners?
- What is problematical in my partners?
- What is supportive in my relationships?
- What is problematical in my relationships?

When you have explored and thought over your answers you might then be able to consider:

- What should I be looking for?
- What should I be avoiding?
- What aspects might I be aware of?

You have a lot more choice and control over your relationships than you might think. Now is the time to recognize that and resolve to turn it to your advantage in the future.

How to make depression work for you

A common reaction to becoming a single parent, usually coming on some time after the actual event, is depression. A good dose of tearful melancholy can work wonders – crying is actually a positive and helpful act as it produces feel-good hormones, which is why we feel relieved and often refreshed after a weep. But depression is another thing entirely. Depression is energy-draining and leaves you feeling exhausted and often unable to make decisions or take action. What it can do, however, if you can recognize that it has struck you, is provide the impetus to ask for help.

Don't be ashamed of being overwhelmed

There is no shame in either being overwhelmed by the difficulties that have struck you or in developing depression, which is a recognized medical condition. You'd be superhuman if the situation didn't knock you sideways, and depression is very common. If you haven't already begun to access the wide range of help that is available, depression is the signal to do so.

Your family doctor should be the first port of call. GPs can offer medication to tide you over for a short time. But the best, most effective and long-term help for depression is talking therapy – counselling. Your GP can refer you to appropriate support teams and organizations, and Mind can provide leaflets and suggestions (see the Taking it Further section at the back of this book for more information).

How to make bargaining work for you

The problem with bargaining is that it stops you getting on with the real work. Also, the bargains you strike with yourself may be harmful and punitive, such as promising to give up treats such as a night out, or personal developments such as a college course or a new job if fate will somehow make your situation better. What you can do is bargain with yourself and fate, in productive and positive ways.

Ask yourself 'What do I want?'

Ideas storm what you would like to happen in your life in the future. Ideas storming is an excellent technique to use when you want to break out and think of new ideas, or old ideas in new ways. When you ideas storm, you ask yourself a question – in this case 'What do I want for myself and my family now and in the future?' and then write down every single idea that pops into your mind. For the first section of ideas storming, you don't censor or criticize – you put it all down.

Begin big. Picture all the things that would make your life exactly the way you'd like it to be – a lottery win, having a millionaire with perfect looks and personality fall madly in love with you … go to town!

Then get a bit real – list all the more sensible and reasonable ideas. Imagine the life you could live, with some effort and imagination. It may seem a very long and almost impossible journey, and it would be unworkable if you thought you could only do it by jumping from where you are now to where you want to be (from A to Z, so to speak) in one move. The trick is to break it down into small, manageable steps. Realize that what you're trying to do is go from A to B, then B to C, and so on.

Sometimes the crazy idea you might have thrown out turns out to be one that might help you on your journey. By the end, instead of having an impossible task that you'd only achieve with a magic wand, what you should have is a shopping list which may take some time, but can be done. Patience and persistence are key.

How to make acceptance work for you

Sooner or later, you will wake up one day and realize that you have let go of the fantasy that it was a mistake, that going back was your only solution, and the guilty belief that it was all your fault. You'll have reached the best place, where you accept that what has happened has happened and that you can't change the past. With acceptance comes real resolve and understanding – that while you cannot change the past, you can change the future. And you will be ready to take charge.

> **Essential points**
> - Understanding your emotions – especially understanding the role of anger and how you may deal with it – can help you come to terms with being a single parent.
> - Becoming a single parent can involve painful losses but it also involves some gains. Using the process of coming to terms and reflecting can help you make resolutions for a better future.

Telling the children

While you are struggling to come to terms with becoming a single parent, your children may be doing so too. As loving parents we strive to protect and guide our children. When family change occurs, two barriers can come between us and helping them as best we can.

The *first barrier* is that you may be so overwhelmed with your own needs that you take your eye of the ball as far as your children are concerned. Your own confusion and unhappiness may take over. In such a situation, we often feel that one way of keeping control is to keep everything quiet. Not discussing the issue, refusing to consider it out loud or ignoring it feels like a good way of making it go away or at least holding it at arm's length. You may be so caught up in managing your own panic and misery that you actually forget that your children are part of the picture too.

The *second barrier*, and the reason your children may fall under your radar, is the belief many of us have that the best way to protect children is to keep them shielded from anything that might harm or confuse them. This is an admirable theory but sometimes unrealistic in practice. **Protecting your children is sometimes counter-productive.** The point is that while you may hide what is happening from your children, you can't shield them from your reaction to it. When children see a parent distraught or worried but don't know why, it's infinitely more worrying than when they have an explanation. And it's highly unlikely you will be able to hide your feelings from them.

What then happens is that you shield them, not from the sadness but from its remedy. By keeping quiet you pass on to your children the message that something has happened that isn't to be talked about. You don't speak, and neither do they. What they may do, however, is try to make sense of it by themselves, and that's when they come up with the explanations that make sense to them – that it's *their* fault, that the other parent left because of something *they* did.

What should you tell them?

You simply cannot keep the truth from them. Sooner or later they will find out – usually far sooner than you think. And if you don't tell them, someone else will. It may be with malice – someone from their school or neighbourhood, who wants to tease or bully them. Or it may be a neighbour, friend or family member who wishes to be supportive and sympathetic.

When considering what and when to tell them, it's best not to assume that what you have to say is a total surprise. However well you may have thought you had hidden your disagreements or unhappiness, and however young they may be, children aren't stupid. Check out with them what they have understood so you can proceed from there.

Case study

When Tracey and her husband Dave decided their marriage was at an end he moved out and went to stay with his parents who lived a mile away. Tracey felt it was too soon to tell their three children, who were 12, 8 and 5 years old. Dave would come round before the children were up to see them over breakfast. Since he worked as a long-distance lorry driver they felt his not being there over weekends and evenings could be explained by saying he had to work, and he came some Saturdays and Sundays to take them out and some evenings to kiss them goodnight. Tracey noticed that all the children, particularly her eldest son, seemed to play up a lot more but put it down to the fact that she was tired and stressed. Until, that is, during one particularly painful row with the boy he burst out 'I want to go and live with Dad!' Tracey was stunned and said nothing but talked it over with her best friend who was appalled she hadn't told the children what was happening. Tracey had felt the children could contain their grief and confusion if she kept quiet, but later realized that their saying nothing was making it worse. That weekend, she and Dave got the children round the kitchen table and told them, together, that they had separated. Everyone cried and it was a painful experience, but all hugged and kissed and the children could ask the questions they needed answering – was it their fault, would Dad come home if they were good, would he go on seeing them? Dave promised in future to ring them every night if he wasn't going to be there, and the children's behaviour improved.

When and how should you tell them?

Children need to be told what is happening as soon as possible, as clearly as possible and as truthfully as possible. But equally, they need to be left out of the anger and the fault finding. The main important points for you to convey to them are:

- Mum and Dad are no longer living together.
- We don't love each other enough anymore to be able to live together but we still love you.
- This is not because of anything you did – it's not your fault.
- It's okay to cry, to be sad and angry.
- We may be upset with each other but we're not upset with you.
- You can love both of us equally.

- We both love you and you'll be able to see both of us.
- (in the event that the other parent won't be in touch) Dad/Mum won't be around but it's not because of you.

Follow up telling them by asking them:

- What would you like to know?
- What would you like to say?

Listening to what your children have to tell you and responding to the questions they have is just as important as telling them what you think they ought to know.

When you tell your children that your relationship is ending or has ended, you need to keep two important things clearly in your mind.

1 **Do not to confuse honesty with being inappropriate.** Children need to hear the truth from you and need to be able to ask questions and have their own feelings appreciated and heard. They need to know what has happened and why and what is going to happen and why. They need to know the unadorned truth and not lies or fantasy. They need to be reassured. But the things they emphatically do not need or want are to be used as weapons and caught in the crossfire.

What shouldn't happen is for them to feel responsible for your feelings, either for the existence of them or solving them. Your children, even when they are grown up, are your children. They are not your best friends, 'like a brother or sister', or as adult as you. You may think that they are big enough to support you and are capable of being leaned on, but it's positively damaging to your child to have to 'parent' his or her own parent. Leaning on or relying on your kids and telling them that they have to look after their brothers or sisters or you, or that it's their role now to 'be the man/woman of the house' leads to confusion and difficulty, both in the immediate situation and later, either when you make a new relationship or when they come to make their own.

2 **Recognize that you won't be telling them once and then putting the whole issue away.** 'I don't want to have to tell you twice!' is not a helpful phrase to use with children about anything, because children frequently need to revisit the things you tell them, especially when it's about changes and distressing matters. You'll need to discuss the matter again with your children, many times. Just as with that other taboo, sex, separation is not an issue that children can process in a

one-off lecture that settles the matter once and for all. **Your children will need to revisit what you have said again and again.** Even teenagers need to go over it repeatedly. Young children may want to go back to the subject even more. They will need to know what it means for you and what it means for them. However painful or difficult it may be for you, it's important to recognize that the ending of a family can't be wrapped up and disposed of in one short burst of activity, just as a relationship cannot be consigned to history and forgotten about in a moment. You may need to deal with it with your children slowly and with repetition.

Who else should you tell?

Once you have told your children – and they should be the first to know – the next task is to tell other people. Who should you tell? There are four categories:

1 Those close to you
2 Those close to your children
3 Organizations and authorities that need to know
4 Other contacts.

Those close to you

Those close to you are your support network – the people who will stand by you and support you. You may think first of family, or of friends. Whatever, both need to be told. If they're close, they may not be surprised to hear the news – indeed, the people who love you may have spotted the warning signs when you did not.

Have a clear idea of what you need and want from people. In their desire to support you and your children, friends and family can sometimes do or say things that you may like to hear but that in the long run are less than helpful. Chief amongst these is any criticism against the other parent. This may seem to be what you want to hear, but such denigration carries penalties. This is your child's other parent. Whatever you may think about them and whatever they may have done, your child needs to hear good things not bad things about their parents. So say to your friends and relatives:

- I'd really like your support.
- No badmouthing my child's other parent, please.
- What I'd really like is…

Friends and family might welcome some specific and concrete ideas for what they can do for you – you might need a night in with friends, a shoulder to cry on, a babysitter so you can get out, help with shopping or DIY – make a list and help them to help you with the things you actually want.

Those close to your children

Your family will obviously be on this list but there may be some people that form your child's support network who you won't turn to straightaway. First amongst these would be your child's other grandparents and relatives.

Even when a parent may want nothing to do with their child – or, of course, in the case of bereavement when they are no longer there to be able to do so – their own parents, the child's grandparents, may have no such barrier. Neither may other relatives – uncles, aunts and cousins. They need to know, and in as low-key a way as possible, that any animosity will be kept out of all future contact between you, them and the child.

Your child's friends and their families also need to know. The situation may affect contact with them – arrangements may be broken and the child may be upset – so their knowing what is going on will ensure that there are no misunderstandings. You may want to support your child in telling their friend, but it's your responsibility to tell the adults.

Organizations and authorities that need to know

Your child's school, your doctor and dentist, bank, employer and tax authority need to know. In effect, anyone with whom you have business needs to know, as does anyone your child deals with – youth club workers, health workers, sports clubs. They all need to know so they won't make remarks or ask questions that cause offence or pain, can support you in any difficulties with practical arrangements and can be sensitive to your child's needs.

Other contacts

There are many people with whom you and your child come into contact, such as neighbours and your colleagues. You may feel that they have no business knowing about your private life and you may be right. The only issue to consider is whether they may hear about what has happened and whether it may affect how you, they and your child cross paths. If you think there is any possibility that what they think, say or do about this situation could be uncomfortable, it may be better to be proactive and put your own spin on it. Gossip that goes on behind your back has potential for great harm. Information that you give out and thus control can be used by you for you.

Summary

- There are 1.8 million single parents caring for 3 million children in the UK, and 10 million lone parents in the USA, so you are not alone in being a single parent family.
- Coming to terms with your single parent state is an involved process with many emotions to go through and deal with. Don't expect it to happen overnight.
- The stages to pass through – shock, denial, anger, guilt, depression and bargaining – can all be turned around and made to work for you.
- Don't allow friends or family to offer a 'quick fix' solution for your new situation. Ask for help and support in finding your own solution and use techniques like reflective listening to help you make the most of this.
- The main question to ask yourself is 'What do I want?' Using the ideas storming technique can help to get you the best answer to this.
- You cannot change the past, you can change the future. The sooner you fully accept your new state, the sooner you can move on.
- Tell the children, and everyone else concerned, as soon as possible. 'Protecting' them by keeping things secret is often counter productive. If you don't tell them in your own words, someone else will and you could lose your children's trust in you.

Be positive. Single parents do a good job – just as good as two-parent families.

02

getting over feelings of guilt and failure

In this chapter you will learn:
- how to deal with the myths about single parenting
- how to overcome guilt and value yourself
- how to reduce stress
- how to produce an action plan
- about making time for yourself and getting your needs met.

Starting again

Becoming a single parent can be stressful and exhausting. The initial shock may be bad enough, with all the pain and tension of realizing you're on your own. You may take some time to come to terms with the simple recognition of what has happened. But one day you wake up, take a deep breath, and acknowledge that this is where you are. You're a single parent and you're going to have to get used to looking after your children and making a life without your ex-partner. That's when the real work begins. That's also when the real fun and joy can begin and that is what this book is all about: helping you achieve the best for yourself and your family.

What is the greatest drain on a single parent's reserves?

If *becoming* a single parent may be stressful and exhausting, *being* one can be even more so. You have so many more calls on your time than when you were a couple. Even if your partner didn't pull their weight around the home, in the relationship, or in the family, they were still a presence. Having to do the jobs of two people by yourself as well as trying to keep a home and perhaps a job going as well is no joke. But the physical demands are often less than half the story. The greatest drains on your resources are the emotional ones. Not only may you be battling with a crisis in self-confidence and self-esteem, with anxieties over your competence and capabilities, but you may also be fighting other people's image of what it means to be a single parent.

The myths of single parenthood can make you feel bad about yourself. It seems every time the issue comes up in the media, instead of being sympathetic and supportive of a family struggling with loss, or a parent valiantly battling on to do the best for their children, the picture presented of single parents is that they're selfish or spongers. You may be alarmed to see judgements on children brought up in single families: suggestions that they are disadvantaged and doomed to inevitably leave school without qualifications and follow the pattern of early parenthood and broken relationships. Worst of all is the impression that a single parent is a failure for not keeping a marriage or a relationship intact and that broken families mean broken lives. This chapter is about fighting back against those myths and reclaiming the positive aspects of being a parent and being an individual. Because the good news is that once you can take control, you will find that being a single parent can have as many positive sides to it as being part of a two-person family.

How to deal with myths

In fact, the best way to deal with myths is to **ignore** them. If someone insults you or puts you down, it's not your responsibility to put them right. It's your responsibility simply to live the best way you can. But since the myths do depress and worry most people, you need two forms of reassurance. Firstly, to know the myths are just that – stories with little basis in truth. And secondly, it helps to raise your own self-esteem and confidence so that you don't begin to believe them.

How to deal with the myth you're selfish

It's hard to credit how you can be selfish if, as mostly happens, your single parent state was not your choice. It may have been your decision to call an end to a relationship that had soured and a family situation that was unhealthy for all of you, but the circumstances that led up to that are unlikely to have been what you might have wanted. Would it be any less selfish to decide to stay in a relationship that had, to all intents and purposes, ended? We sometimes talk in terms of couples 'staying together for the good of the children' but does that actually do children any good? Children may not have experience but they do have intelligence and the ability to understand what is going on about them. Living with parents who do not love each other is a very harmful experience. Seeing conflict, even if it is hidden, is confusing and injurious for them. Watching a relationship lacking in love or respect gives children terrible messages about what relationships are all about, and very low and detrimental expectations for their own relationships, now and later in life.

But introducing the whole idea of whether bringing children up on your own is selfish or unselfish is beside the point. Couples who stay together can do so for very 'selfish' reasons. Indeed, when you really examine motives, very few people act entirely altruistically. The truth is that parents, on the whole, do their best for their children and single parents are no different. How you got to where you are now is not the point; how you are going to manage for the best for everyone, including yourself, is.

To the myth that being a single parent is selfish you could say *'I'm doing my best for my children, just like any parent would hope to do.'*

How to deal with the myth you're a sponger

Single parents of young children are often presented with a perfect Catch 22 or double bind. If you stay at home to be a full-time parent and look after your children, you will be accused of being a sponger, especially if you claim any form of benefits. If, on the other hand, you go out to work you will be accused of having 'latch key' children who lack a parent's firm hand and who will soon go off the rails.

As a society we put value on people who earn money. Indeed, they way we assign value to people is through the amount of money they have in their pay packet. We still value people with vocational jobs such as nurses and fire-fighters even when they are not paid as much as they probably deserve, but virtually anyone making lots of cash is assigned a high status. Conversely, someone not earning much or none at all is given a low status. Non-earning parents seem to be way down the list even though what they do is potentially the most important job there is – bringing up the next generation. As a society, we should be nurturing children, our future, and thus supporting their parents to do a good job. This is why we have a system of care and benefits available: benefits financed by money collected from us all, for the good of us all. If you are in receipt of help now, that help is coming from those in work at the moment. But in a few years' time, you will be one of those people paying into the pool, as you might have been a few years ago. You're not a sponger, you are collecting what is rightfully yours as a member of this society just as, as members of this society, you and your children will someday make your contributions.

The reasons that some people get trapped in long-term unemployment are complex and diverse but invariably parents want to contribute as well as they can towards their children's future. Chapter 09 looks in detail at what may be available to you to raise your skills and expectations if you're not working and would like to, either now or in the future. But for now, ignore the label of sponger because it isn't true.

To the myth single parents are spongers you could say 'We all contribute to society in different ways at different times.'

How to deal with the myth your children will be disadvantaged

Single parents often look to the stories they see in the press and the statistics often quoted that appear to support the idea that children from single parent families will be badly affected by being in such a family form. Headlines tell you that children from single parent families are more likely to be school truants, do badly in exams and have fewer qualifications, be involved in antisocial behaviour including drink and drug use, engage in early sexual behaviour and become single parents themselves.

What is true is that family breakdown can hurt and harm children. When children sustain painful losses that are not dealt with or understood they often 'act out' their pain and anger. This will be explored in more detail later but for now the point is that what leads to problems with children from a single parent family is not the break-up of their previous situation and their being in such a family, but how you handle it. If children see an acrimonious break-up with continuing conflict, if they feel caught between warring parents, if their unhappiness and need for explanations and security is not addressed, they may well react adversely. If on the other hand the arguments stop, if children know they are loved, cared for and valued, if they can ask questions and have them answered, they have exactly the same chance of fulfilling their potential as children in two-parent families. Indeed, they have better outcomes than children stuck between unhappy parents in an intact but discontented relationship. Single parents do as good a job as parents in a two-parent family – and often a lot better.

To the myth your children will be disadvantaged you can say 'My children know they're loved and their parents are there for them. That's the best support for any child.'

How to deal with the myth that your children will inevitably follow your lead

The children of teenage mums and the children of single parents are more likely than the general population to follow their parent's pattern. But again, you have to explore why this may be rather than seeing it as an inevitable consequence of the situation. One possibility is that since children love and not only wish to emulate but forgive their parents they may show you what they think by doing the same. In effect they are saying 'You did well by me' in the clearest way possible. Another reason is that it is, after all, the model they grew up with and even though you may have said 'This is not what I want you to do', children are more likely to do what we do, not what we say. We learn how to be parents from our own parents, after all. Being in a family that shows it can do without a second parent can have children concluding that this is the way it is and should be.

However, just as with any other influence, most of it is picked up from the unspoken assumptions that are flying around in the family. These are issues you could directly control by bringing them out into the open. The more parents and children communicate, the more you discuss and analyse and thrash over, the more authority you have over what choices all of you make.

To the myth your children will follow your lead you can say '*My children will have love and attention from me and will make their own choices in life.*'

How to deal with the myth you're a failure

Being a single parent still has a stigma attached. It's often seen as the worst situation a person can fall into, a dead-end disaster zone. Part of the bad reputation of being a single parent comes from having stopped being with someone else. There is still the feeling that being one half of a couple is 'better' than being a singleton. If you're a couple, you've been chosen and picked and it shows you have worth. When a relationship ends, however this happened, the assumption is that someone failed.

If your relationship fails, the chances are that in the middle of your pain and distress you will be asking yourself 'What did I do wrong? How was I lacking? Could I, should I, have done anything different? If I'd been better looking, harder working, funnier, cleverer, would my partner have stayed?' As well as all the exhausting practical details a single parent will be struggling to manage in the early days of being on their own, they will also be struggling to cope with self-doubt and a crushed sense of self-worth as they think about how they failed to keep the other parent of their children by their side.

Relationships fail without people being failures. They don't always turn out the way we would like them to. One of you may have held back from getting truly involved with the other or perhaps one of you may have let your attention and commitment slip over the years. Whatever the reason, fault and blame are not helpful concepts.

But while it may not have been your fault, it could have been at least partly your responsibility. Sometimes, the partners we choose or the way we approach relationships can mean that we may be more likely to find it all ends in tears. If you can see a negative pattern emerging, it may be the time to consider whether you should look at the patterns and make some changes. Asking for help from a counsellor might be what you need. But equally, what happened may well be about the other person's demons, not yours. Having a relationship fail makes you a human being, not a failure. For now, what you do need to do is build up your self-esteem.

To the myth that you're a failure because you have had a failed relationship you can say *'Some relationships last and some do not and that's just life.'*

From the postbag

My wife left me to go off with my best friend and to say I feel terrible is an understatement – I feel crushed. Our two children are with me and I'm keeping going for their sake but my mind just keep going round and round on what I could have done to make her stay – and what I can still do. Doesn't she know how much I love her? If I could only make her understand it, maybe she'd come back. How can I tell her I love her and the children need her and she has to come back to us?

I'm sure you've told her and I'm sure she knows. Sadly, while you may think the force of your own love and need should change another person's mind if only they could feel it, the truth is that she has her own feelings and needs and that's what she's listening to, not yours. You can certainly make it clear that for the moment the door is open and you'd welcome her back but you may have to accept that while you still love her, she has made another choice. You and the children would be far better off dealing with what you've got – a home with the three of you who need to make the best of it. And there is a lot that is good and hopeful. You have them and they have you. They are the ones who really need to hear from you how much you love them and that you will be there for them, whatever happens in the future.

They also need to know that none of this is their fault and that though Mum and Dad will not be living together, she still loves them as much as you do, and will be in contact. You need to shift your focus from the need to make her listen to you and return home to letting her feel she can be in contact with the children without your putting pressure on her. Good luck!

What is self-esteem and what builds it?

Self-esteem is knowing that you matter. It means that you feel worthwhile and confident, able to deal with problems and manage your life. Someone with self-esteem knows they are as important as anyone else and deserve to be valued and cared for.

We build self-esteem in others and foster it in ourselves by:

- valuing and accepting ourselves and other people
- respecting, caring for and loving those close to us
- accepting respect, care and love from those close to us
- listening to others and asking them to hear us
- taking time, with other people and ourselves.

Children learn to value themselves if we value them. Your self-esteem may have already been low in your relationship. Perhaps you've been unlucky enough to have lost out in your own childhood and had an upbringing that did not foster your self-confidence. Or you went into your relationship with a good opinion of yourself but arguments and tension have left you feeling low. Self-esteem goes down when the people we care about denigrate us and are heedless of our feelings and opinions. Self-esteem goes up when our feelings are acknowledged and our needs are met – both by ourselves and by other people. **Value yourself and other people will too.**

Valuing yourself

Being a parent is a hard job. The pressure we often put on ourselves to do it perfectly can make it worse. Sometimes we stop valuing ourselves because the expectations we have are unrealistic. We may say to ourselves:

- *I ought to be more patient*
- *I can't put my feet up – I should be cleaning the car*
- *I can't play now – I have to clean the kitchen*

Every time you do something for yourself you feel bad, as if you don't deserve it, and every time you have the impulse to take some time for yourself, you fence yourself in with 'oughts' and 'shoulds'. It's really important that you make time and put in effort to relax and feel good about yourself. Next time you find yourself saying you ought to do something, or can't do this or that, or should be doing such-and-such, stop yourself dead. Ask yourself 'Who says?' 'What stops you?'

Reducing stress

'I ought to...', 'I must...', 'I should...' are all messages that make life stressful. And while stress can be helpful and get us going, it can also exhaust and put us on a knife edge, ready to blow.

- Go easy on yourself. You don't need to be perfect – there is no such thing as a perfect parent. Being good enough should be your aim.
- Do some things just for yourself – some exercise, some relaxation, some time alone. You'll return to being a parent refreshed.
- Do the things you have to, not the things you feel you 'ought' to, and reserve some time for the things you want to do, too. If you can make time for the important things you can make time for yourself. You are, after all, important.
- You feel stressed when you feel out of control. So take control of the things you can and you'll feel better.
- If you're feeling tired, upset or stressed the chances are it's because you need something. Get your needs met and you will regain control.

Essential points

- Becoming a single parent is stressful and exhausting, both physically and emotionally.
- The myths so many people believe about single parenthood can make you feel bad about yourself.
- Raising your self-esteem and self-confidence can help you fight back against your own lack of self-worth and other people's pressure.

Being positive

The most important and effective strategy for living life to the full as a single parent is to put a positive spin on it. There are many elements that make your life after a separation different from how it was before. But for every drawback you may come up with there is an advantage. You may feel rejected and a failure for having had your relationship disintegrate. This isn't a *failure*, it's a *transition*. Finding that one relationship no longer fits is a prelude to others.

It's not that you couldn't make it work, it's that in common with many people, you found that yourself and your relationship moved on. Sometimes what was right for us when we were one age simply doesn't fit a few years on. It's sad – especially sad when there are children involved – but looking forward is better than trying to go back.

Putting a positive spin on it would mean looking at the way you may describe how you are now, and reframing it to see the upside rather than the downside. So, you aren't 'abandoned' or 'left behind'; you are 'ready for something new'. You aren't 'on the shelf'; you are 'mature and experienced'. Sit down and write out all the negative statements that occur to you that describe your situation and your life after separation. Then rewrite every single one with a positive slant. Do it with a friend or a family member and you may find yourself in fits of giggles at the ridiculousness of it all. But you could discover that depression and despair are really a result of looking at things in a downbeat way. You could start feeling more positive if you approach it differently.

How to come up with a plan of action

Putting a positive spin on the way you see your separation and life after separation is also a way of coming up with a plan of action. Your list of all the problems and drawbacks of your life will show you where you may want to make changes. For instance, you may put down:

- I feel lonely, isolated and alone.
- I feel unsupported.
- There is no one who can back me up.
- No one cares or understands.
- Making ends meet is a problem.

- Having full responsibility for childcare is a burden.
- I don't have a job that earns enough money.

From your list you can see the areas which you will want to change. What you could write down from this might be:

- I need to get in touch with old friends and make new ones.
- I need to call on my friends and relatives more for support.
- I should look to local and community support schemes.
- I should investigate what helplines or organizations there are nationally and locally to help me.
- I should ask for help from the relevant organizations in managing my finances.
- I should find out what childcare is available to me.
- I should investigate training and further education.

Whether you want to talk to someone who understands or get help with practical matters such as training, job opportunities, financial advice or meeting new people, there will be people and an organization that can help you. What is needed is for you to take the first step of deciding what you want, picking the ones that can be of help and then approaching them. You have to do the work in taking the actions that they might suggest but they will have done a lot of the hard work already by researching and having at their fingertips the questions you need answering and the areas you'd like to work at.

Fighting your anxieties

We all have anxieties and moments of doubt. That's the time when you can be affected by people's opinions, or your perceptions of them. Looking at the skills and abilities, strengths and qualities that you have both as a parent and as an individual, and how these are going to help you move forward in providing a secure and loving family environment for your children to grow up in, can help you fight back. Try this exercise as an opportunity to reflect on what you have achieved and what you will achieve. All parents achieve a huge amount – single parents often more than others. All it needs is for you to recognize what you have done already and what you can do from now on. But you might also need to recognize when your expectations are unrealistic – that the standards you set for yourself cannot be fulfilled and are unreasonable.

Expectations exercise

Sit down with a pad of paper and a pen. Ask yourself:

1 What do I expect from myself?
2 What do I expect from life?
3 What do I expect from a relationship?

The things you might find yourself putting down could be:

1 What do I expect from myself?
- I should always be competent, strong, in control.
- I should have a partner – if I don't it means I'm a failure.
- I should know how to meet new people.
- I should be a perfect parent.
- I should keep a perfect home.

2 What do I expect from life?
- Life should be fair.
- People shouldn't let me down.
- My family should love me, no matter what.

3 What do I expect from a relationship?
- I'll be safe and loved.
- I'll always have someone to care for me.
- I won't need any other people but my partner.
- It will last forever.
- It will never change.

When you've added your own ideas, think them over. Are your expectations realistic? Where and when did you learn to expect these things? Are your expectations helping or hindering you to move on? And most important of all, if you changed your expectations would it help you?

Making time for yourself

Being a parent or carer is a really important and difficult job. As a parent, you often spend all your time looking after everyone else in the family and leave yourself to last. Looking after yourself is a way of valuing yourself, and if you want to raise your self-esteem and confidence, one of the best ways of doing that is to take care of yourself. If you want to give your children what they need from you, it's vital that you look after your own needs too. It can be difficult and painful to give other people what they need if you feel that nobody looks after you.

It's like sharing a cup of tea or coffee. If your cup is empty, when somebody asks for a sip you have to say 'Sorry. There's nothing here for me, so nothing for you.' If your cup is half full, at least you might be able to let them have some, although that leaves you with a depleted store. But if your cup is full you can say 'Of course! I have plenty – drink your fill!'

It's easy for you to be overwhelmed by your family's needs and for your 'cup' to get emptied very quickly. If you're running on empty, you have nothing to give to yourself and nothing for the other important people in your life. This can leave you feeling worthless and useless, and all of you feeling resentful and angry.

Looking after yourself isn't being selfish. It's being aware that you're important too and deserve to be cared for just as much as anyone else. And that the better you feel, the better you can help other people feel too. You owe it to yourself, your family and the others in your life to do things – even small things – to make yourself feel good. Every little treat helps to 'fill your cup' so you've got something to give out. It might be:

- sitting in the garden
- walking the dog
- having a bath
- listening to music
- reading a magazine or book
- doing some exercise
- going shopping with a friend
- planning a holiday
- emailing or phoning a friend
- watching a favourite TV programme
- meeting a friend for coffee or a drink.

Take some time to work out what makes you feel looked after, cared for, rested and refreshed.

Case study

When Sanjay's wife died and left him with their three children, he negotiated with his employer to work more from home so he could take them to and collect them from school, and work flexibly to cover illnesses and holidays. A year after his wife's death, Sanjay was taken ill by a winter virus and spent most of the Christmas holidays in bed. Since his parents had already planned to come and stay they looked after the children and finally persuaded Sanjay to see his doctor, who fortunately looked at the whole situation rather than simply his physical health. It became very clear Sanjay was exhausted, physically and emotionally. He had been so keen to show he could manage that he turned down offers of help from friends and relatives. More importantly, his entire focus had been on the children, to his own disadvantage. Sanjay never did anything for himself and neither did he allow anyone else to do so. When his wife was around, the children did chores but now he did them all. And he'd given up his Friday night card game with his friends, which his wife had always said was the one treat he owed himself. Under the strict orders of his doctor, and with his mother's and his good friends' help, Sanjay restructured his life to put some care for himself as well as the children in place. Between them they worked out a new chore chart – which the children said they were happy to do as they knew Dad had needed the help. His parents promised to come round every Friday to cook and babysit, and were delighted to do so as were the children, to spend time together. He also accepted some invitations from friends to parties and events. He felt better for himself – and the children noticed a difference too.

Essential points

- Putting a positive spin on the situation can help you to come up with a plan of action.
- Learning to recognize your expectations can mean you make them realistic and helpful.
- Looking after yourself is as important as looking after your family.

How to get your needs met

Make time

There are only so many hours in the day, but that doesn't mean you can't have some time for yourself. Often, the only reason you don't is because you feel you don't have a right to it. *Make* time by planning ahead, knowing it's essential for you and everyone else.

Be realistic

Set your sights too high and you won't attain your goal – and may then feel you can't expect anything. Be realistic about what you expect of yourself and everyone around you and build up from there.

Ask for help

From now on, you'll let other people know directly and clearly what you would like and when you want help you'll ask for it. When people offer support, you'll say 'Thanks! That would be a great help' instead of thinking 'I can't accept – it would show me up.'

A sixteenth-century clergyman and poet called George Herbert once said '*Living well is the best revenge*.' It's one in the eye for anyone you may feel has let you down as it shows that you can manage perfectly well, thank you very much. It's also the best way of fighting back against your own anxieties and concerns and the 'bad press' – to use everything at your disposal to make sure you look after yourself and your family. George Herbert also said '*Storms make the oak grow deeper roots*.' This experience, however unhappy and difficult it may seem, is a challenge you can rise to. By doing so you will find that you can do more than cope – you and your family can thrive.

Summary

- Being a single parent can be stressful and exhausting. The first step to make to combat this is to get over any feelings of guilt or failure that you may have.

- Part of moving on successfully is to be aware of the harmful myths surrounding being a single parent, to see through them and not let them affect you.
- Self-esteem is knowing that you matter and are worthwhile. Building self-esteem is important for anyone – especially lone parents.
- Stress and single parenthood can go together. Use the techniques given here to reduce yours as much as possible.
- You cannot change the past but you can change the future. Put a positive spin on things, make sure your expectations are realistic and then form your action plan and stick to it.
- Look after yourself, make time for yourself and get some of your own needs met. The more you can take care of yourself, the better you will be able to take care of others. Being 'selfish' occasionally is a necessary part of being a happy single parent.

03

helping your children cope

In this chapter you will learn:
- how to help your child cope
- how to deal with your child's emotions
- about changing your or your child's name
- how to help your child build their own social networks
- how to manage special days or events.

Focusing on your children

Children need to know as soon as possible that you are going to be a single parent family, and will need to ask and hear again and again what happened and why. If they were too young to know when it happened, or if you didn't say at the time, it's never too late and never too inappropriate to go over it now. They need to hear it from you and while they need reassurance and comfort, they also need to hear the plain, unadorned truth. They need to hear:

• Mum and Dad won't be living together anymore.
• This isn't going to change – there won't be a last minute or later return.
• It's not their fault.
• You love them and are there for them just as much as ever.
• Their other parent still loves them, will be seeing them and is still there for them (if this is appropriate).

It is sometimes difficult to recognize and acknowledge that children may have a different take on the situation than we do, and that may prevent clear communication about what has happened. For a start, children may harbour the fantasy, long after it is in any way reasonable, that their family will come back together again. Even if their other parent left when they were too young to know them and has never been in touch – or indeed is dead – child may dream that it was all a mistake and will be put right. Even children in happy, intact families sometimes daydream that they're actually a long-lost prince or princess and that one day their real parents will reclaim them. Children missing a parent can become convinced that one day they will be swept off to a fairy-tale ending.

Helping children make sense of contradictory feelings

You may be heaving a sigh of relief at having escaped from a bad and destructive relationship which harmed you and your child emotionally and maybe even physically. You may have mourned, but with a few weeks' or months' perspective you have perhaps arrived at a point when you can see it as a positive move, and one you are glad happened. Your children may never see this as a situation they welcome, or they might see the positive aspects but have difficulty in managing something that does need some experience and maturity; to have two contradictory feelings and balance them. One advantage of being grown up is that we know we can be angry with someone and still love them. That we can see the drawbacks of something enough to know we shouldn't do it, and still long to do it. Children can find this split very confusing. When they are angry and disappointed with a parent who they also love, they often react by deciding that it is wrong to have such 'bad' feelings, thus thinking that there is something wrong with them.

Helping children cope with 'bad' emotions

We do tend, in this society, to divide emotions and feelings into 'good' and 'bad'. Good emotions might be love and contentment; bad ones might be envy, jealousy or anger. When children are behaving well because they are experiencing the 'good' emotions they tend to get praised – they learn they are gaining approval not just for their behaviour but also for feeling that way. But when a child experiences one of the 'bad' emotions and behaves accordingly they tend to get told off. What they then learn is that not only is it not acceptable to behave badly but also that it isn't acceptable to be angry or jealous or envious. Early on we learn that having a bad emotion makes us bad, so eventually when we feel a negative emotion we may want to deny we're feeling that way or make excuses, or blame someone else for 'making' us feel like that.

Children will feel all sorts of very negative emotions around them being in a single family. They may feel angry at the parent with whom they stay for letting it happen, angry at the parent who has gone for having abandoned and rejected them and jealous of people who are with the missing parent. They may resent siblings more than ever, for being there and taking up some of your precious attention, which feels to them as if it's stretched to breaking point. All these emotions need to be dealt with and managed or they will spill out in arguments, sulks and conflict, making everyone unhappy.

No 'good' or 'bad' emotions

The way you cope is by realizing that there are no 'good' or 'bad' emotions – only emotions. All emotions are normal and natural. You can't help having them. What you can help, of course, is what you do about them. But if neither you nor your children are given the opportunity to voice these feelings, they will remain underneath the surface, bursting out as difficult behaviour.

We need to allow children the chance to voice negative feelings and fears. It may seem like a good move to only voice the good bits, and to accentuate the optimistic view. We can do this with ourselves, to set our minds on looking forward and to see the positive side of our fears and anxieties. But before you can get to that point with children – and yourself, actually – you first need to hear their real emotions. What can you do when your children come to you with anger and pain, which you may not want to take on board? Take a deep breath. Remind yourself that you're the adult. Listen to and acknowledge what might be underneath their emotions.

• When they say 'I hate you!', do not say 'No you don't', instead say 'I can understand that you're angry with me.'
• When they say 'You spend more time with him than me!', do not say 'No I don't', instead say 'It sounds as if you're saying you'd like more time with me.'
• When they say 'It's not fair!', do not say 'Life isn't fair', instead say 'I know that you wish things were different.'

Acknowledging painful, difficult emotions takes the sting out of them, and then allows you to go on and deal with them. Sometimes, simply making it clear that you hear and understand is enough.

How much do you tell your children?

There is a fine line to tread between giving children all they need to hear, and too much information. Children need to know that you are going to be a single parent. They need to know how it is going to affect them and what they can do about it. They need to know where they stand with the other parent. They do **not** need to know the ins and outs and the details of what happened between you and the other parent.

When you consider what you might disclose to various people, recognize that there are degrees of appropriateness. You may spill your heart to someone such as your own mother or father, but hold back on certain intimate details that your parents simply do not need to know. You may tell those to a friend, but hold back on some other details you'd trust to your mum – especially the things that might show you up in a bad light that you'd hate a friend to know about but that your mum knows anyway. And there are things you might tell a therapist – you'd probably give them the fullest account. But what you tell a child – even a teenager – should fall short of all of this. A child is neither your parent, your therapist nor your friend. They're a child – someone you love and trust and hope will tell you enough to let you care for, guide and protect them. But that's the key: you are the carer, guide and the protector. It isn't a two-way, mutual relationship. You're the adult and while you should give them the information they need and the honesty and frankness they deserve, you are the one who has to hold the painful, messy details to yourself.

Leaning on your children (or not)

Similarly, when it comes to asking for practical help as well as emotional support, there is a fine line between the healthy and the inappropriate. Helpful relatives and friends will often mistakenly try to boost a child's morale and give help to the parent in the aftermath of a separation by telling children they are now their parent's support and mainstay – 'You're the man of the house', 'You'll have to be mum from now on'. The child may be urged to be a substitute for the missing parent or a confidant for the parent on their own. This can actually be confusing and counter productive. Children encouraged in this way can be burdened with adult responsibility far too young and put in positions with their siblings and their parent that are far from comfortable. You do not want to refuse the help and support they might offer since that would be demeaning, but neither do you want to make them look after you. Children in single families need to know their support and help is required and expected, but it is the help and support you'd expect from a child, as in any family, not a friend or parent.

It helps for them to know when you're sad, angry, or feeling low. They can sense it anyway, and when you are feeling below par it's often impossible to function as if everything was fine. So they suffer from the consequence of your emotional state – if they know how you are feeling they can understand it's not that you're upset with them. A simple 'I'm not feeling too good at the moment. In fact, I'm sad/angry/feeling low but it's not your fault. Bear with me!' is sufficient – don't go overboard and divulge everything to them, remember that they are not your friends and confidants.

How children can support you

One important aspect that children most certainly can help with is keeping the home running. While being used as a domestic servant would not be at all fair, children not only should but would actually be proud to be depended on to do some work in the house. Depending on their age they should:

- help around the house – laying tables, doing washing up
- clear up their own mess – mugs and plates after snacks, clothes and toys
- keep their own room tidy and make their bed
- look after family pets – feeding, exercising, cleaning up.

The key to keep in mind is that all of you should be helping each other to feel safe and secure, supported and listened to but that no one should feel dumped on or taken for granted. As a part of that, get into the habit of telling your kids how much you love and value them, just for being them. Not because they do their chores, not because of what they do but because of *who they are*. In the middle or the backwash of a break-up, it's easy to forget to keep saying 'I love you!'

Essential points

- We can't help what we feel but we can help what we do about it.
- There are no 'bad' or 'good' emotions. Emotions are emotions – all are normal and natural.
- You need to strike a balance between keeping your children in the dark and giving them too much information.
- Children benefit from being asked for their help and support but not from being leaned on or treated like friends or parents.

How should children tell other people?

Children may need your help in explaining their family circumstances to other people. There are obviously people with whom your children interact that are your responsibility to inform, such as school authorities or health personnel. But there are also contacts of your children who fall into their sphere – their friends. You may be the one to tell their friends' parents, but they may need to consider passing on the information themselves rather than leave it to be given over second-hand.

You can help them by rehearsing or 'role playing' telling other people about their family. Discuss with them what they want to say:

- My mum and dad are no longer living together.
- It wasn't because of anything I did – it's not my fault.
- Sometimes I feel sad and angry about it. If I do have an 'off' day, it may be because of that.

Either:

- My mum and dad both love me and I see mum/dad regularly.

Or:

- My dad/mum isn't around but it's not because of me. My mum/dad is there for me all the time.

If children feel confident about what to say and that what they know is correct, they can recognize that there is no shame in their situation. If anyone does try to see the fact that they are in a single parent family as an excuse for teasing or bullying, their response can be like a shield. '*Yes, my family is single parent. So?*'

Changing your name

Single mothers who were married to their child's parent or who had taken to using his name might want to change their name after a split. You may wish to revert to your maiden or original family name, or the name you used before that marriage. Or, you may wish to choose an entirely new and different name, to signal a step into the future and away from the past.

If adults want to change their family (or indeed, their personal) name, it can actually be very simple. You don't have to go through any legal procedure or involve the courts to do so. Anyone can call themselves anything they want, as long as there is no intent to defraud or commit any offence but you cannot give yourself a title by adding 'Sir' or 'Lady' or call yourself by the name of some famous person with the intention of having people assume you are them. But if all you are seeking to do is change your name (to lose a personal or family name you no longer want, or gain one you would like) all you need to do is start using the new name and tell everyone it is the name you would like to be known by from now on.

You need to tell anyone who needs to get in touch with you or has any dealings with you that your name is now different. That means not only telling your friends but also informing any organizations so they can change their records to show your new name. Amongst others, these would be your employer, bank and credit card companies, GP and dentist, the passport agency, the DVLA, your mortgage company or landlord, your local authority and your child's school.

Some authorities and organizations will simply accept a letter from you explaining that you have changed your name. Others may ask for more proof. If you have gone back to your original name, simply show your birth certificate. If you have returned to a previous married name, show your old marriage certificate. If your change is to something new you may need to provide:

- A Change-of-name statement. In this, you state the old name, the new name and have someone witness and sign it. Some solicitors can provide, or you can download from the internet, a statement like this for a small sum.

- A Statutory Declaration. This is a Change-of-name statement that has been witnessed by a magistrate or solicitor. It may cost a bit more than a simple Change-of-name statement but it still not very expensive.

- Deed Poll. The most expensive option. This is a formal document that needs two witnesses. You can 'enrol' the deed poll, which means it is published in a weekly government publication and the information is kept safe in the Central Office of the Supreme Court. You would need to pay to have the document drawn up by a solicitor and another fee to have it enrolled. But you can choose to simply have it drawn up, signed and witnessed and then you keep it to show anyone who needs to see formal proof.

How a name change might affect your child

If you wanted to go ahead and change your name you would need to consider your child's reaction and, if they were old enough, to understand and talk it over with them. Children, even if they keep the name they've always used, can be profoundly affected by your making a change. They may feel that you're rejecting the last link with their other parent – a link they need to keep and may need to feel that you have to keep too. They may feel left out and abandoned if you take on a name different from theirs – as if you were cutting some ties with them, as well. And they may feel confused about who you are and where your loyalties lie if you have not only a different name to them but a different name to the one they've always known. Even with a young child it may be necessary to sit down and ask 'How would you feel if...?' and to hear and take on board what they say, even if it makes uncomfortable listening for you.

Children, of course, may want to keep the same name as they have got used to. They may find it embarrassing and difficult to have a name different from yours but still feel attached to the name they have known as theirs. Or, they may make a strong case for abandoning the name to be in line with you. Their underlying motive for rejecting the name may be one of anger, hurt and loss – a way of striking back at a parent who is no longer there and saying 'Keep your rotten name – you don't want me so I don't want it!' Sometimes children make this move when they feel the parent is withdrawing and it's a way of taking control, of getting their rejection in first so it may not hurt as much when they are abandoned. Sadly, the result sometimes is that the non-resident parent feels they are no longer needed or wanted and the withdrawal becomes complete, when it may not have been so. But sometimes it may be a reflection of the situation – that it was a name that has no meaning to them because there is no contact or identification with it.

If there is no contact with the non-resident parent, a name change for the children is something you can discuss. But it is worth considering what a change might actually mean. If they did change, would that prevent any question of connecting with their origins? Are you in contact with grandparents and other relatives from that side of your children's family and would it mean they felt they no longer had a connection? There can be no hard and fast rules on this – what would be best for you and your children is something you need to work out. But above all it is the children's best interests, and their interests over the long term, that matters. If the courts do uphold a request for a child's name to be changed and it is to one that is different from the one on the birth certificate you cannot change the certificate to match – that will continue to show the original surname.

How does your name change affect a child's name?

If a name change would result in your child having a different name from you, you may want to reconsider. Name changes for a child under the age of 18 can be more complicated than those for adults. Strictly speaking, you can change a child's family name in exactly the same way and with as little fuss as an adult's. It all depends on what name is on the child's birth certificate, whether you are in touch with the father and whether he has certain rights.

If you were married, you may find that your child has to keep the married name – even if the father is no longer in contact and even if the child wants to alter it. If a non-resident parent objects to name change and takes it to court, the court is likely to uphold the request for the family name to remain as it was. If this happens there would be a court order – a Prohibited Steps Order – to prevent the name being changed. Even if the parent has no contact and so is not around to object, the courts may still rule that the child should keep the name they were born with. The reason for this is that an adult has every right to sever the link they had with the adult with whom they no longer want to share a name. Partners, in other words, can divorce. A parent is a parent for life, however, and children often desperately need that tie, to remain either in contact with their parent, or at least with their own past, and thus themselves. It's bad enough losing a parent, the family as it was and a sense of family being something stable and secure. Losing your name on top of that can be a step too far, even when the child feels they would like this to happen.

If, however, it is your maiden name on your child's birth certificate and you either want to stop using a name you had simply taken up, as had your child, both of you could go back to it, since that is both your and your child's name anyway. Similarly, if you wish to adopt an entirely new name and to have your child follow suit, if the father does not have Parental Responsibility (see Chapter 04) this is your decision.

Case study

Deirdre's parents divorced when she was 3 months old and her mother moved from South Africa to the UK, reverting to her maiden name. There was no contact at all with Deirdre's father. Deirdre continued to use her father's name, the name on her birth certificate, until she was around 6 or 7 years old when she became distressed at the number of times she was being asked why she had a different name from her mother. After a tearful discussion, Deirdre began to use her mother's name, telling her school and doctor that this was what she wished. When she applied for a passport at the age of 9, her mother wrote a letter explaining why her name was different from the one on her birth certificate and this was accepted. Since then, she has always used her mother's maiden name and it is on all her official documents. Only when she has to produce a birth certificate does she need to explain why it is different.

Fostering children's social networks within the family

One of the best ways of helping children cope with your being on your own is to encourage them to develop their own strong social networks. Children need to feel connected in order for them to weather the anxieties that their family is vulnerable. Children need to have free access to family members such as grandparents, aunts, uncles and cousins. If possible, they need access to family from both sides, even if interaction between you or the child and the other parent is hostile or non-existent. Since children cannot be expected to manage contact you need to facilitate it. This means making arrangements for meetings, organizing travel if necessary and generally helping the child to feel this is normal and okay. It may feel like a burden to you – hard work, expensive and a waste of time – but the child doesn't need to hear that. Even teenagers, who can and often should make their own arrangements, may need support to keep the connection going.

If children show distress at the idea of seeing family members, not just in saying they don't want to see them but in 'acting out' with sudden illness or seemingly unrelated bad behaviour, talk with and listen to them to find out what is causing their reaction. It may be that:

- they feel disloyal to you
- every time they see family it reminds them of the separation and that saddens them
- a family member is being unpleasant about you or someone else the child is fond of
- a family member is putting pressure on them over something.

Anxieties of disloyalty need discussion and reassurance. You may need to stand back and put aside your own quarrels for the sake of what your child needs – unfettered contact with the people who mean something to them.

A reaction to having intermittent contact is common. Children often play up and become miserable before or after seeing a non-resident parent or their family. You may conclude that it's the meeting that makes them upset and want to limit or stop them altogether. In fact, the pain is about the parting not the meeting. Every time they know a meeting is coming up, they know a parting is too. And every meeting only underlines the fact that they are apart from people they love. That's why they may get moody or angry or sad. The remedy is not less contact but more.

Family members may find it hard to resist doing things they feel are supportive of 'their own' – such as criticizing or bad-mouthing the other people in the situation. Children may find this confusing and very painful. You may need to be in touch, to calmly and carefully say:

- I understand your feelings
- You have every right to your feelings and opinion
- You have every right to express your feelings and opinions in private
- Please don't express them in front of [the child] as it upsets them
- Let's make an agreement that we do not criticize or complain about each other in front of [the child].

Encouraging children's social networks outside the family

As well as contact with family, children need their own friends. Even small children make close friendships at school and in their neighbourhoods, if allowed. Parents need to make it easy for children to see their friends, even when it takes time and effort – and even when you may not be so keen on the people they choose to be with.

Making friends is part of working out who you are, and allows children a measure of control and choice. Children in single families may feel part of their life is very much out of their control – they didn't choose and may not want to have one instead of two parents at home. They may need to have the option of selecting friends to give them a sense of power. And for that reason, they may well opt for people you don't like.

Part of this may be to get up your nose – to say 'You've done something I didn't want, so now watch me do the same to you!' All teenagers rebel – it is part of being a teenager, and this may be a natural extension of that. Or it may be that they see something important in someone – loyalty, imagination and courage – that they need and you can't see. Perhaps the friend has been through a similar family upheaval and is a kindred spirit. It's fine for parents of pre-school or primary school children to arrange 'play dates' with people who are their friends to get their children together, and these can become close playmates. But you also need to ask who they might want to see, and respect and trust their judgements and requests, making as much effort to take them to see those children and asking them round to your home as you do the friends you might have chosen.

Once they get to secondary school, all your efforts to stop children seeing and being friends with the people they choose are likely to be frustrated. And, of course, will tend to make the other child even more attractive. After all, what the child will be defending is their choice and taste as much as the other child. Look and ask yourself:

- Why does my child want this friendship?
- What may they be getting out of it?
- How can I best help and protect my child?

Listening to their views and talking it through is more effective than laying down the law. We'll look in Chapter 06 at ways of conveying your anxieties and asking your child to talk with you when they do things you would rather they stopped.

Managing festivals and family events

Festivals and family events can be painful times for children in a single family. They may see how their friends celebrate them, with two parents and lots of family around them. They could be seeing this idyll through rose-tinted glasses, but the point is that they may feel disadvantaged in comparison. If they used to have family festivals with another parent present, any subsequent event may be tainted with regrets and loss. Discarding traditions you used to share may be a source of pain. They may want to cling to them as a way of recalling and keeping in touch with the past. Or, they may furiously reject anything that brings to mind other times or seems to belong to a parent who has rejected and abandoned them. With several children you may find one defends while the other rejects a tradition. You may also find they are running on different emotional timetables – some up when others are down. You may need to:

- be aware of negative as well as positive feelings about the festival
- be sensitive and sympathetic to sudden emotional storms
- recognize several children may mean several different feelings and reactions
- be flexible and spontaneous
- allow them the chance to 'chill out' on their own during the event.

Holidays and festivals are an important part of being a family. Celebrating them together says 'We belong to each other.' So you'll want to make them as special and as memorable, and as much 'yours' as any other family does. Small families, even families of two people, are just as much a family, and can have all their own fun and traditions. To put together the best event for your family, ask your children:

- What would make them sad about the event?
- What would make them happy about the event?
- What traditions would they like to keep?
- What new elements might they like?

Use their answers and the subsequent discussion to create a festival that pleases all of you and helps them feel a positive link to the past is maintained, while providing a bridge to the future.

Case study – Liz's story

Did I miss out, being in a single family? When I was growing up it was just me and my mum – my dad died when I was four. And all my grandparents were dead, too. But I never felt I missed out. My mum used to take me into central London every Christmas Eve – I can't remember when we started doing that, it seemed we always did it. We'd walk around and look at the lights and the shop displays – some of the big ones had fabulous dioramas every year on a different theme. We'd buy hot chestnuts and stop somewhere for a hot drink. By the time we'd get home I'd be so tired I'd go to bed with no arguments and always wake up to a stocking full of presents and oranges and chocolates. The main presents would be downstairs under the Christmas tree and there'd always be one from Dad, even long after I believed they came from him. We'd have presents before and after breakfast and then go out for a walk. Then we'd make a big lunch – we'd always have to have Christmas pudding and cream afterwards but since neither of us liked turkey, each year we'd have a different roast. Then we'd play games and cards and end the day watching a film on TV. And we did exactly the same thing right up until I left home for university. Before I got married I spent some Christmases at home, and when I did it was the same routine. And it wasn't Mum insisting on it, it was both of us. So I now have children of my own, but Mum comes for Christmas and we still do exactly the same – a walk round town on Christmas Eve, stockings in bed and presents under the tree, a walk and a late lunch. Oh – and Mother Christmas sneaks into our bedroom and leaves me and my husband stockings too. No, I don't think I missed out at all.

Helping children feel good about themselves

When children have one parent they can feel insecure. Whether if in their memory there was only ever you, or if they can remember their other parent being there, they may wonder if losing one parent could mean another might go too. If they experienced conflict and saw arguments between you, they may fear that raised voices and angry feelings could be followed by another loss. If the other parent died, they may wonder if every little cough and cold could herald further tragedy. All children need to be reassured that their parents love them unconditionally, but children in single parent families may need it especially. Whatever their age, children need:

- **Protection** – to be kept safe
- **Love** – to be cared about and valued
- **Respect** – to be listened to and given choices and responsibilities they can handle
- **Comfort** – to be kept warm, fed, clothed and healthy
- **Attention** – to be noticed and have time spent with them
- **Stimulation** – to be have plenty to do and think about.

Giving children what they need is **not** the same as:

- **Always putting them first** – you have needs, too
- **Doing everything for them** or giving them everything they want – sometimes they need to wait, or make some effort, or accept that they can't have what they choose.

You can't protect your children from all unhappiness or problems and it wouldn't help them if you could. Children learn to cope with sadness only by facing up to it and managing to deal with it. Try to protect them and what you actually do is shield them from learning how to overcome their problems. Being able to enjoy the ups and get through the downs will help them make the most of life, as a child and as an adult. Spending time with children and paying attention to them makes your life, and theirs, easier and happier and gives them the resilience and the skills to deal with the bad times as well as the good. Your children will feel secure with you and their self-confidence will be enhanced if you:

- schedule special time with each of them – do something with them you know they really like

- spend time together as a family – always eating meals together and having games nights
- ask their opinions and advice
- give them appropriate responsibility
- tell them you love them and like their company
- give them a sympathetic listening ear whenever they need it.

Particularly when children hit the teen years, we tend to think that they rely on friends or other role models more than parents. But in fact, parents are a crucial influence on their children – what they experience, what they become and achieve and how they manage the times when they feel alone, rejected or marginalized. Statistics suggest that the children of lone parents do worse in life opportunities. But that isn't because of being in a single parent family. It's because being there is usually a result of loss and pain, and it's how you manage the loss and the pain that makes the difference. You can give your child as good a start in life as a two-parent family – and indeed, a far better one than many families. All you need are the strategies and suggestions in this book to help you do the job you want to do.

Summary

- There are no 'good 'or ' bad' emotions – only emotions. The key to helping your children cope is to understand and accept the contradictory emotions that they may have about their situation.
- It's important to strike a balance between telling a child too much and keeping them in the dark.
- Children should play a part and be a help in their family, but it's inappropriate and unhelpful for them to be leant on or used as confidantes.
- It's your responsibility to let other people know about your new situation and it's important that you do, as soon as possible. Your child will need your help and support to tell their own friends as well.
- Family festivals and events are important to single families. They may be a reminder of loss but they are also opportunities to pull together and celebrate who and what you are.
- Changing your or your child's name can have considerable significance – it may be desirable for you but you need to consider how any name change might affect your child.

- Children need their own social networks, and need you to help them make and keep them.
- You cannot protect a child from unhappiness and difficulties but you can help them to cope by making them feel good about themselves.

04

going it alone

In this chapter you will learn:
- who can be there to support you
- about non-resident parents supporting their children
- about mediation and counselling
- about Parental Responsibility.

Alone but not alone

There are plenty of upsides to being a single parent. But, let's face it, you wouldn't be reading this book if everything in the garden was rosy. This book is here to address the difficult issues, and to help you find a way to manage them. So let's look at one of the hardest parts of being a single parent – the fact you have no one to lean on. When you've had a hard day, when one child won't stop singing and the other won't stop shouting, when neither will do their homework or go to bed, in a two-person family you can throw up your hands in despair and hand over to the other. Once you have got them settled for the night you can collapse on the sofa together and have a whinge. You can joke and laugh and pick each other up. Being one of two means there is someone else there to share anxieties and the load, to divide the work between you. It also means there is another person to share the fun, excitement and joy of parenting and to give you an adult voice and an adult perspective.

As a single parent you're alone in the home. If you don't manage the quarrels, insist that homework must be done and teeth be cleaned, or prepare the evening meal, no one else is going to do it. What is far more difficult is the fact that you have no one with whom to compare notes or moan about the problems, or reflect upon the triumphs. It's not just that you have the whole workload that two-parent families divide in two. It feels like more than double the burden because the whole emotional weight is on you as well as the entire practical responsibility.

At least, that's how it might seem. The reality is that there is plenty of help and support available, if you go out and look for it. You do have to seek it out because it's not 'in-house' as a partner would be. But it is there, nonetheless.

This book!

For a start, this book is here to support you, with encouragement, tips and strategies and plenty of ideas for you to make use of. Most of it is common sense, all of it comes from years of my and other people's experience and some of it is, I hope, a revelation. The main message is that **you can do it**. It's the situation that makes it hard, not incompetence or incapacity on your part; and a little effort now will make such a difference in the very near future. The very fact that a book has been published to help you shows, above all, that **you are not alone**, and that there are solutions.

What could your family offer?

Your first port of call should be your family. If you have parents, siblings, aunts, uncles and cousins they may all be delighted to help in some way, if you ask. If you've had some time as a two-parent family you may have got out of touch with family members. If you didn't need their help and all of you were caught up in running your own lives, contact apart from the big festivals might have lapsed. It's also possible that you could have drawn away from them because of differences of opinion or lifestyle, or even arguments. You may now feel too embarrassed to call on them, or are afraid that they may rebuff you.

But what's the worst that could happen? That they say no, which leaves you no worse off than before. The more likely result is an enthusiastic welcome. They may not have come forward themselves to offer help because they thought it would be disrespectful. If you've put up a front – as most people do – of managing perfectly well, they might have felt that since you seemed to be coping on your own there wouldn't be any point in sticking their noses in.

Family can offer babysitting or a chance to share days out. They may also be happy to take your children out for treats or even regular outings, leaving you time to catch up on the things you'd like or need to do. If your children have cousins around the same age you may be able to find after-school care or weekend play dates with them, to give you time to work or do essential home jobs. They can also offer a listening ear if you want to ring up late in the evening for a grumble and a chance to put experiences side by side. Grandparents and siblings with families have been there themselves and would understand your concerns or worries and you could either have the reassurance of hearing someone say 'Oh yes, they did that too and I felt exactly the same!', or together come up with solutions.

What could your friends offer?

Friends can also offer babysitting and shared days out. One idea you could suggest to several friends with children is that you form a co-operative. You could meet up at one house, for instance, on Saturday and several of you mind the kids while the rest take the opportunity to go shopping or whatever you would like or need to get done. You could agree that one or two of you take lists and shop for the group, which:

- gets round the nightmare of shopping with children
- allows you to take advantage of two-for-one deals.

Other times all of you could go out together, sharing the task of keeping an eye on the children. Children over quite a wide age range will not only play happily together, they like and benefit from learning how to interact with different ages. And sometimes you could swap babysitting duties. Obviously, there is an issue with single parent families – it's not as if one of you can stay home with your kids while the other goes and watches someone else's. But you can arrange sleepovers where they drop off the children to stay with you and vice versa.

Friends can also be on the end of a phone when you need them. We all have moments when we're close to breaking point. If you have a 'phone buddy' and both of you know the other will be there no matter what with sympathy and the chance to cool down, it would give you confidence to manage those nights on your own.

- Ask for help. If you don't ask, you don't get because nobody knows your needs.
- Have a range of people to call on so you don't outstay your welcome with any one.
- Be specific about what could help – babysitting, a chat over coffee, childcare advice.
- Be specific about how often you'd like their help – this one time, once a week, once a month.

What could an organized group offer?

There are organizations and charities that offer support to families. There is also a range of groups that can offer self-help and friendship for parents, with some specifically for single parents. You may not be a 'joiner' and feel perhaps shy about going along to a new group when you don't know anyone. It's worth making the effort – they are immensely useful.

If your child is four or under and you're in a Sure Start area, they give help to families and can also refer you to local groups and parenting support. There should be a Children's Centre offering a wide range of services and support to families with a child under five in all areas by 2010 – there may be one in yours now so ask through the local school or Sure Start. Home-Start UK is a charity that visits parents with child under five and gives practical help. Meet-a-Mum association puts mums who are lonely and isolated, especially if suffering from postnatal depression, in touch with each other. One Parent Families with Gingerbread and SPAN (Single Parent Action Network) have local groups especially for lone parents with children of all ages.

Groups such as Sure Start and Home-Start and MAMA focus on toddlers and some are there with practical help with issues such as postnatal depression. Gingerbread and SPAN have local groups offering friendship and activities for parents of children of all ages. But all let you know **you're not alone**, and most will give you contact with other parents so if your social group has become a bit sparse, this can help you make friends, and friends with a lot in common. Please see the Taking it further section at the end of this book for details on all these organizations.

What could the internet offer?

The parenting charity Parentline Plus, as well as their 24/7 helpline, has message boards on its website (**www.parentlineplus. org.uk**) that allow you to get in touch with other parents, as does Mumsnet (**www.mumsnet.com**), Parents Centre (**www.parentscentre.gov.uk**), UK Parents Lounge (**www.ukparentslounge.com**) and Parents.com (**www.parents. com**). All offer online communities (see Taking it Further for more details). They are there for all single parents but Dad.info (**www.dad.info**) and Singlefather (**www.singlefather.org**) are there particularly for lone fathers. If you have access to the internet, online groups can offer an always on-call network of other parents and single parents to give you encouragement and practical ideas. They can sometimes be there for you when your friends could not – at 3 a.m., for instance. And they can also cope with the issues you may feel embarrassed about raising with people you know as you can go online (or use a helpline) anonymously.

What could your local community offer?

If you can't find a local group, you could form your own. Gingerbread and SPAN can aid you in setting one up. As well as organized parent and child groups, your local community could offer you plenty of opportunity to meet other people who would be like-minded or in a similar situation to yourself. You could bump into other parents at family activities – your child's clubs or sporting events. You may see them on a bench in the park, at the swimming pool, watching their children play, or in supermarkets, coffee shops or food outlets. Parents might nod at each other or pass a few remarks in such circumstances, but many get chatting and soon become friends. If you're not the natural 'chatty type', practise and perfect the skill. Most people would welcome new friends and just like you are delighted to make new allies. It just takes one of you to make the first move and suggest coffee together.

Contact with the non-resident parent

For every single parent there must have been another parent. You may be a single parent because of bereavement – in which case the following section sadly cannot apply to you. Or because you're a mum who decided to go it alone and have had AID – artificial insemination by donor – in which case, the biological father is not available to be a parent. In some cases, the non-resident parent may be out of contact and makes no attempt to be in touch so, again, isn't on hand to be a parent. They may have said they want nothing to do with you or your child, they may simply have absented themselves. Indeed, you and anyone you know who knew them may not even know where they are or what has become of them. But under any other circumstance, there is another parent who should be fulfilling their responsibilities to your child. If this parent is around, before you dismiss this idea, read on.

Children's reaction to contact after the separation may increase the pressure on non-resident parents. Often children act badly when they see the non-resident parent. Or, the resident parent has to cope with challenging behaviour as children are moody or argumentative before and after visits. Both parents may conclude that it's the visit that is at fault and decide that if they were curtailed the behaviour may improve. Non-resident parents often walk away for that reason above all – they may feel that since children 'act up' so much around contact visits it must be because the child doesn't really want to see them, and it might be far better if they dropped out of the scene and let the child and other parent 'get on with their lives'. Even parents who walked away carelessly can regret doing so. Parents who do so, thinking it is for the best, often suffer dreadfully.

While some non-resident parents are mothers, the fact is that the majority are fathers. And part of the problem is that all of us, and men in particular, do not have a positive image of what it means to be a dad and how important that role might be. 53 per cent of fathers and 42 per cent of mothers agree with the belief that the father's role is to 'provide'. 'Being a man' is seen as 'having a job'. 'Defending the family' is considered as the main job for dads rather than 'being a good father'. This means that when men are not the main earners in their families, they do not value their place as parents. Once a man has left the family he (and all around him) may feel he has no place in it and no function to fulfil. If he does want to remain a father to his children, he may go along with the view of his role as being the defender of his family and fight for his rights in court, rather than negotiating it in a conciliatory way to avoid conflict. This may result in an entirely hostile atmosphere that eventually makes the resident parent feel contact is far more trouble than it is worth.

Why do non-resident parents lose touch?

In most cases, non-resident parents do not stay away because they don't care about the child; or, indeed, the resident parent. If the relationship ended in anger, bitterness and open conflict, both parents may hope to draw a line under what happened and move on. Seeing or talking to each other only brings back the unfinished business they have between them – the unresolved arguments and quarrels. Neither may feel they were able to put their case across to the other and be heard, and both may feel there is no point communicating with someone who won't take their views on board.

What may be lost in the hostile atmosphere is the need to step back and recognize that the needs of the children are separate from the needs of the adults. You may still have a quarrel with the other parent but you have no quarrel with the child, and it is the child who suffers when a parent goes missing.

The sad fact is that many fathers only really value their family, and are motivated to make efforts to be with them, when they lose them. The majority of non-resident parents do have regular contact and are involved with their children. Two-thirds of non-resident fathers pay maintenance and seven out of ten have regular contact with their children. Nearly half of children see their non-resident father at least once a week. However, a third of children only see them once or twice a year. One reason may be hostility and obstruction from the resident parent. The humiliation and pain, the feelings of rejection and abandonment that accompany the end of a relationship can result in continuing antagonism. This is often expressed in making contact hard. Arrangements will be changed or broken, arguments over money may result in withdrawing contact, children may be sent on or back from visits with a list of grievances. Eventually, contact may dwindle and cease.

Why should non-resident parents stay in touch?

Whatever the reason for the break up, unless the non-resident parent has been judged as being a danger to their children, contact should be maintained. Whatever fathers may think of their role in a family and with their children, children have no doubt: they value fathers as much as they value mothers. And research supports their view, that dads are important. Where fathers are involved in their children's lives, children's well-being is higher and they are more protected from mental heath issues. A father's interest in his child's schooling is strongly linked to good educational outcomes for the child. Fathers and mothers do offer different strengths and different skills to children. More importantly, a loving relationship with both gives children self-worth and self-confidence. Children need contact with both parents because:

- It tells them who they are. You don't have to explain genetics to a child – they know instinctively that they are a combination of Mum and Dad. If one, or both, birth parents are missing children feel rootless and cut off. They may also feel anxious and apprehensive about what surprises and booby traps may be waiting in themselves, left there by the missing parent.
- If they don't have a clear idea of why the parent isn't there, they may well try to explain it themselves. And children's fantasies about loss usually revolve around their own blameworthiness. They'll believe it was something they did or didn't do or that they were weighed and found wanting. They'll believe that the parent left them, not that they left either the other parent or the relationship, and so feel rejected.
- They need to feel a parent's approval and acceptance. Losing touch with a parent feels to a child like having that source of appreciation and recognition withdrawn and often results in a lack of self-esteem, self-confidence and self-worth.

This is not to say you cannot manage very well on you own as a lone parent – you can. Lone parents who have to take on the role alone are as capable of bringing up children with strong self-confidence and self-worth as those in two-parent families. But you do have to address the worries and concerns that children may have about why the other parent isn't there, and if you have a choice it's much easier when both parents are in their children's lives.

The resident parent can value the contact as well. If the non-resident parent is functioning as a co-parent, the 'lone' parent is not as alone as they might have been. If you can accept and acknowledge that your relationship as partners is over but your relationship as parents goes on, you can be there for each other in this capacity. The big barrier to this is that to let your child's other parent in, you have to give up your exclusive relationship with them. You have to acknowledge that while you may feel they were a lousy partner, they can be a good parent. Your feelings and needs, and your special status, has to take a back seat. The advantage, of course, is that it means you are not alone. Face-to-face or at the end of a phone you have the other half still, available for a chat or a moan about *your* kids – theirs and yours.

Helping non-resident parents to be co-parents

1 **Ask for help and see doing so as a strength not a weakness.**
   Resident parents often shy away from asking for the other parent's help because of pride. They want to be seen as managing and the parent who left them, or they left, is the last person to whom they want to lower their guard. Pride is a good thing when it is positive. In this situation it is self-destructive and harmful to the child, who would really benefit from having their other parent's place in their life recognized and acknowledged.

2 **Help your child's parent recognize their strengths in parenting.**
   While both sexes can offer exactly the same in the essential functions of parenting – unconditional love and approval, a desire to keep children safe and secure, a willingness to listen and respect, a willingness to play – men and women do bring different aspects to the table. Children benefit enormously from having the love, attention and care of both a parent of the same sex as them and one of the opposite sex. Single mothers need to recognize and acknowledge the part fathers can play in their child's life. As a whole, more fathers are becoming hands-on and active parents and are spending more time with their children. In the mid-1970s, fathers of under fives spent less than a quarter of an hour a day in child-

related activities. In the 1990s this had increased to two hours a day. Fathers, mothers and children all benefit from this.

3 **Honour their skills and what they have to offer and what their children need from them.**

Non-resident parents, particularly fathers, may lose touch with their children because they have little confidence in their parenting skills and little feeling of self-worth in what they can offer. Dads are not always engaged and involved in their children's lives, seeing their role as caring for the family by bringing in an income rather than getting involved in emotional issues. This can become worse if they are the ones to live apart. Some Sure Start centres have 'Dad and children' sessions that could be particularly helpful for re-engaging fathers. They can allow fathers to recognize what is demanded of parents caring for children, so enlisting their sympathy and resolve to support the resident parent. And it can make the bond between them and their children stronger, and allow them to learn and practise parenting skills. Some schools run 'Bring your dad to school' sessions to get dads engaged and involved – again, particularly useful for non-resident dads. Organizations such as Fathers Direct and the website **www.dad.info** can support and inform fathers who live apart from their children, encouraging them to keep in touch with them, and to go on being supportive of the other parent. For the sake of your child it is worthwhile making clear just how valuable the non-resident parent is to the child, and to you as a co-parent.

4 **Recognize that communication is the key and that talking problems over can reduce conflict.**

Whatever the circumstances of the split, parents who live apart should put aside their own quarrels to care for their children. This may mean opting for mediation or counselling to settle the arguments, and agreeing ways of discussing any issues in the future without conflict.

5 **Insist that your child's school and health carers involve the other parent.**

Non-resident parents can drift out of touch if they don't feel included in their children's lives. One way of making it clear, to them and everyone else, that they are an ongoing part of these children's landscape is to ask all the authorities that care for your child and who may contact you about that child to recognize that the child has two parents who live apart.

Ask that dual reports always be sent, to the two addresses. Some schools are now using technology to keep parents in touch, using web-based reports and text and desktop alerts on school issues and if a child is not in school. These initiatives can help separated parents keep in touch with their children, no matter where they are.

6 Accept that for the other parent to do better, you may have to lose out!

This may be the hardest aspect. Although being a single parent is a tough job – exhausting and wearing – it is also immensely satisfying. Being on your own with your children means you and they have a very special, close relationship based on it being you and them against the world. Letting the other parent in can diminish that. You may fear that letting the other parent have contact can lay your child open to risk – either actual risk of harm, or risk of being let down and abandoned once again. You may have good reason to have this anxiety – or it may be that it is your own fear of being left all over again that it actually the issue. It is hard continuing to have contact with someone you loved in such a situation. You do need to separate your own feelings from the needs of your child.

When agreeing contact, you may like to discuss some ground rules for both of you to keep to:

- No arguments in front of the children.
- No belittling or insulting each other either to the children, when the children can hear, or when anyone else can hear and pass it on to the children.
- No using the children to get back at the other by, for instance, changing arrangements or sending messages through them.
- Recognizing and acknowledging the importance of contact to the children.
- Communicating in a positive manner and striving to make it work.

You may also like to consider the benefits of asking for professional help, either to agree the ground rules of contact, or to allow you and the other parent to settle your disagreements once and for all. You might do this by going to mediation, or by asking for some counselling.

Essential points

- Being a single parent means a lot of work for you – not only is there no one to divide up the responsibilities with, but also no one to share in the fun.
- There are people you can lean on – family and friends, organizations and groups.
- Whether you like the idea or not, your child's other parent is a source of help and support.
- Fathers often only get involved, or ask for help, when they lose their children rather than valuing their family while they are within it.
- Fathers often fight for contact after a separation instead of negotiating it, making children pawns in a continuing struggle with an ex-partner instead of valuing their children and themselves as fathers.

Mediation and counselling

Mediation and counselling are very different things. Counselling is about looking at yourself, your emotions and reactions. It helps you to understand why and how you feel and why and how relationships break down and is a good way to help you look at the unfinished business caused by the end of your relationship. With counselling, an ex-couple could look at what led to the break-up and how they feel now, and be helped to have a final say and know the other has heard it. Counsellors are objective and do not take sides, supporting both parties to communicate and come to an agreed conclusion. Counselling can take anything from two or three to twenty sessions to help you deal with the situation you need to resolve and is entirely confidential. Your own GP may have counselling available in your surgery or you may need to find a counsellor through Relate or through The British Association for Counselling and Psychotherapy. The costs may vary from free of charge to £25-£65 a session depending on income and area. See Taking it further, at the back of this book, for more information.

Children also often need support and help in the aftermath of a family break-up. You can ask for specific help for them through your own GP or through some schools. Or you could consider family therapy so all of you could get some help together – see Taking it further for details.

Is mediation more practical

Counselling often involves painful heart searching and a willingness to be open and honest with yourself and the person with whom you're being counselled. You may not want to do that when a relationship has broken down, but need to at least agree certain things between you. That's when mediation can come in. A mediator can help all of you see eye to eye over contact arrangements, money and any other disputes involved in your situation. A mediator may suggest you go on to see a counsellor, if they think you might benefit from talking through your feelings. And a counsellor may suggest you go to mediation to hammer out the practical arrangements once you have come to terms with the emotional issues.

You, the person or people you're wanting to reach an agreement with and the mediator will get together for between one to five sessions, each lasting an hour or an hour and a half. The mediator will help you listen to the other, understand each other's concerns and needs and help you find a solution that suits everyone involved. Mediators do not take sides and do not push their own solutions. They may well put forward ideas and suggestions, but the aim is for you to find a resolution that is acceptable to and workable for you.

Mediation is confidential. Nothing disclosed in these sessions can be used in court, apart from anything said that suggests that someone is or will be at risk of being hurt or if a crime has or is to take place. Mediation can help you agree issues such as contact and holiday arrangements, how you will communicate and maintenance and money.

At the end of mediation, you'll usually write down the main points you've agreed so you can check it's working for you and return to this if there are any later problems.

Mediation is free if you are on a low income or is charged on a sliding sale, depending on how much you can afford. Find a mediator through the Family Mediators Association, National Family Mediation or UK College of Family Mediators – see Taking it further for contact details.

When parents can't face each other

What if you and the other parent of your child simply can't bear the idea of coming face to face? What if there are real concerns about the child's safety with them or someone else in the family? Or what if you find the idea of letting a child go home with the other parent, or other people who know them, unacceptable? In such a situation, a Child Contact Centre could be the answer.

A Child Contact Centre is a place where children can spend time with a parent who lives apart from them, and other agreed family members. Child Contact Centres are run by The National Association of Child Contact Centres and all of them are accredited and the staff and volunteers are fully trained. Families are either referred by a social worker, solicitor, mediator, The Children and Family Court Advisory and Support Service (CAFCASS) or a court order. Or, at some centres, you can refer yourself. You apply by filling out a form, naming the people who will be seeing the child, and then make arrangements for a visit. Child Contact Centres can offer three levels of support for separated families.

1 Supported child contact

The centre is warm and friendly and will have toys and areas where children can play, and facilities for adults to have refreshments. You take the child there and stay with them until the other parent arrives. You can handover seeing each other but if this is not acceptable you don't need to actually be face to face at any time – when the other parent arrives staff will take the child to them. After handover, children can spend as long as agreed with the other parent and any relatives that have been named on the referral from, in the centre. While there, certain rules must be kept, for the safety of the child and to ensure the visit is fun and safe:

- No arguing in front of children, no abusive or aggressive behaviour.
- Only the people named are to be there.
- Children cannot simply be left – one parent has to handover to the other, even if they don't see each other face to face.
- No drink, drugs or smoking and no one under the influence to be allowed into the centre.
- The parent leaving a child must give a phone number where they can be reached.

2 Supervised child contact

When there are concerns about the risk to the child, or when parent and child have not seen each other for some time and may need help re-establishing a relationship, contact can be supervised. The child and adult are under observation at all times by a supervisor – a highly trained professional – with the support of another colleague. The visit will have a time limit, and reports will be kept to help the supervisor keep the child safe and to support parents in managing the visit in the best interests of the child.

3 Handovers

Most Child Contact Centres will function as a drop-off point, where parents can go and play with their children while waiting for the other parent to collect a child for a planned visit, either for the day or longer. This is useful if you don't want the other parent to visit your home or go to theirs. As with supported or supervised visits, parents do not have to see each other face to face.

Fathers' rights

Over the centuries, children have been viewed as the property of their parents which meant when a divorce occurred, they would fight for 'custody' or care and control of the child, perhaps with the parent who lost the battle being able to retain access rights. The Children Act of 1989 changed this. Instead of rights we began to talk about responsibilities, and instead of custody we began to see what happens after a separation in terms of contact and residence.

At the heart of what the law now says about separated parents is the assumption that parents have equal responsibility for their children and should go on having contact and a relationship with them. This is true whether or not parents were married when the child was born or when they parted.

If parents had a short-term relationship – or no relationship at all – and if parents now wish to have no contact whatsoever, either between themselves or between parent and child, it is irrelevant as far as the responsibilities owed in law by parent to child. An unmarried father is responsible for his child even when he has no rights over his child. So he may have no contact – even be banned from having contact – but still have to pay towards the upkeep of his child.

The courts would now far rather parents decided **contact** (how much time a child may have with one parent) and **residency** (which parent they will live with or whether they will have an equal home with both) between them. When there is disagreement, however, the courts may step in to make or confirm that decision for them.

Parental Responsibility

The key concept with children and parents who live apart is Parental Responsibility. There is no longer any legal difference between children with married or unmarried parents. But an unmarried father does have fewer rights than a married one over his child. He does, however, still have exactly the same responsibilities.

A parent with Parental Responsibility can decide:

- a child's name
- what sort of education they have and which school they go to
- where they live
- their religion
- what healthcare they should be given.

A parent with Parental Responsibility has the duty to make sure the child is:

- safe
- cared for
- educated
- fed and clothed.

Who has Parental Responsibility?

Mothers automatically have Parental Responsibility. So do fathers if:

- they were married to the mother at the time of the birth
- they were registered as the father on the baby's birth certificate, if the birth was after 1 December 2003.

If you have Parental Responsibility for a child you have both rights and responsibilities. It's down to you to look after that child but it's also up to you to make the choices. A parent with Parental Responsibility cannot lose it by divorce or through separation from the child and other parent. Once you have it only a court can take it away and only in exceptional circumstances.

Fathers can acquire Parental Responsibility if they were not married, or did not have their names put on the birth certificate, at the birth. They can:

- marry the mother
- re-register the birth with the mother's agreement to put their name on the birth certificate
- make a Parental Responsibility agreement with the mother.

If the mother agrees, she and the father can sign a Parental Responsibility Agreement that gives him equal rights and responsibilities over their children. If she does not want to do this, a father can go to court and get a court order, if the court thinks the child will be better off if he has it. The court would want to know:

- how committed the father is to his child
- how attached are father and child
- the father's reasons for applying for Parental Responsibility.

Simply being a child's father is not enough for the powerful rights and duties of Parental Responsibility to be conferred – the court will need to know that the father is requesting it because he wants to be part of his child's life, not just as an attack on the mother.

From the postbag

My ex-boyfriend left me soon after our baby was born. He visited now and again but he hated her crying – and she always cried when he held her, because he hardly ever did it and he just wouldn't try to learn how to do it properly. He wouldn't get involved with things like feeding her or changing nappies and after a time simply stopped coming. He's never paid a penny towards her upkeep. Last year I heard he got married and has a little boy. A couple of friends of mine who see him in a group that meets in our local pub say they've heard him say he's going to take my daughter, who is now five, and bring her up as his own and that he can do this because he's now a married man with a family while I'm single. Can he take my child?

He has to have Parental Responsibility to be able to have any say in where your daughter lives, or a Residency Order to say your child should live with him. And since you weren't married when she was conceived or born and this was before December 2003, the only way he would have got Parental Responsibility would have been for you to sign an agreement with him or for him to have gone to court to win it. If he wanted her to live with him now he either has to apply for a Residency Order, which automatically confers Parental Responsibility, or apply first for the one and then the other. The court would have to decide that your child would be better off if he has Parental Responsibility or Residency. And if he's had no contact for at least the last four years and made no attempt to maintain or see his child it's inconceivable that they would. The courts prefer to leave young children with their mothers unless there's a very good reason why she can't cope or is a risk to them. Being single isn't even an issue. It sounds as if he's winding someone up – you, his wife, your friends. Good luck!

A child may only have one mother and one father but can have several people with Parental Responsibility for them at the same time. Grandparents can ask the court to give them Parental Responsibility and may be awarded it, and the resident parent may make a Parental Responsibility Agreement with them or another suitable person to safeguard the child in case something happens to them.

Court orders

The courts don't want to get involved if the situation is settled, or if you can or have worked things out yourselves. So if you're happy about the arrangements made for where your child lives and the contact your child has with the other parent, they will not get involved. But if there is any difficulty, it can be settled in court. The court can make the following orders.

A Residence Order

This is about where the child lives. The courts don't usually take a child, especially a young child, away from the mother. In the heat of a row, a father may threaten to do this but it's not something that happens except for very good reasons. You can have a Residence Order on your own, where it is decided that the child lives with you. Your child may still see and even stay with the father, but you have responsibility for their care. Or, it can be shared, where it is decided that the child is the responsibility of both parents. If both parents share residency, the court may also order how many days or weeks the child spends in each home, or accept your arrangements.

A Contact Order

This is about who the child sees, and might say that the father or other relatives such as grandparents can see the child. It often says how often, when and even where. Contact Orders can also say a particular person should have *no* contact.

A Specific Issue Order

If there is a particular problem that needs settling you can ask the courts to make a Specific Issue Order. For instance, if both parents have Parental Responsibility and disagree on the religion or education of their child, they could ask the courts to say who makes the decision.

A Prohibited Steps Order

This would set out something you don't want to happen. For instance, it might stop someone from seeing your child if you thought they were a danger, or it might say the other parent couldn't take the child out of the country.

What is most important is the welfare of the child. The law recognizes that children come first. They have wishes, thoughts, needs and feelings of their own – and these may be different from their parents. For instance, parents might have separated and never want to see each other again. There may be anger and pain or violence involved. But the child may feel they've lost something important if there's no contact. So the child's rights to have contact as well as the right to safety and security may have to be taken into account. When it comes to feeling alone and unsupported in your parenting, if it's at all possible, the other parent should be your co-parent, there for your child and for you.

Summary

- Be specific about the help you'd appreciate from your family and friends.
- Look for help from organized support groups, your local community services and on the internet.
- Non-resident parents may need support and encouragement to be as involved as much as you need and your children would like.
- Child Contact Centres can be the ideal solution to any difficulties in managing contact between a non-resident parent and child.
- Issues such as Parental Responsibility, Residence and Contact are always decided in the child's best interests.

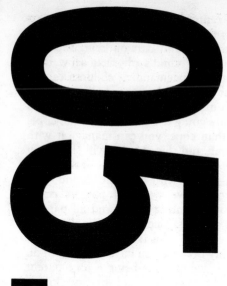

05

parenting tips

In this chapter you will learn:
- about parenting styles
- how to look after yourself as well as everyone else
- how to ACT not react
- about good communication skills
- what children need
- why children might behave badly
- how to get your own needs met.

Being a single parent is like running a three-ring circus on your own. Part of your attention will be on keeping a home going, part on trying to make ends meet and part on being the only one there to cope with all your child's physical as well as emotional needs. Managing lively, demanding children can be hard at the best of times but your kids may be challenging you with their behaviour, and you may be wondering why they do this, and how on earth you are going to cope. But you can cope. Indeed, you can do better than cope, you can manage it with skill and also with enjoyment, and this chapter will show you how. This section looks at the best parenting tricks of the trade, with tips and strategies to get on with and understand your children and help them to behave well. All parents could benefit from brushing up on parenting skills, and all parents can at times feel inadequate and unskilled. Being a single parent may start you off at a disadvantage. This is not because you are any worse a parent but simply because you have so much to do on your own. And whatever led to your being a lone parent may have left you lacking in confidence – and the first skill of parenting is to feel confident.

What sort of parent are you?

Whether we realize it or not, most of us follow a system of unwritten rules and assumptions when it comes to our parenting styles. The way we parent comes from the way we were parented as children. This can be helpful if we were raised with unconditional love and affirmation and can pass it on – not so good if we were left feeling unworthy and lacking. Do you find yourself saying and thinking any of these (tick all that apply)?

1	Do you say *Don't argue with me! Do as I say!*	☐
2	Do you feel *I've got to be in charge or it all falls to pieces!*	☐
3	Do you say *Oh, I don't know – do what you want!*	☐
4	Do you feel *I can't get them to do what I want and anyway, they've had such a hard time...*	☐
5	Do you say *What?*	☐
6	Do you feel *I've got too much on my mind...*	☐
7	Do you say *Don't say that/ask that! We don't talk about such things.*	☐

8 Do you feel *What if they found out? That's such a horrible thing to say!* ☐

9 Do you say *Shut up! Take that! I'll give you something to cry about!* ☐

10 Do you think *I'm furious!* ☐

11 Do you say *I only want the best for you.* ☐

12 Do you think *How can I make it better for them? I'm just not good enough.* ☐

13 Do you say *Do this, darling, it's the best thing for you, I know.* ☐

14 Do you think *I always wanted to…* ☐

15 Do you say *I'm listening, let's talk.* ☐

16 Do you think *I love them whatever but I'll set boundaries for their behaviour.* ☐

If you ticked numbers 1 or 2, 'Do as you're told' may be your style.

Rules will be important to you and they're pretty inflexible. Some parents think they can end an argument by putting their foot down. Yours start out that way.

If you ticked numbers 3 or 4, 'No rules at all' may be your style.

Anything goes and what is acceptable and not acceptable can change from day to day.

If you ticked numbers 5 or 6, 'You've got troubles of your own' may be your style.

You are so overwhelmed by your own troubles that you have very little time or attention left over to engage with your children.

If you ticked numbers 7 or 8, 'Family secrets' may be your style.

There are certain things that you can't or won't talk about. The result is that there are plenty of other subjects that can't be discussed openly, such as emotions or sex.

If you ticked numbers 9 or 10, 'You're so angry' may be your style.

You've had so many bad things happen to you in your life that you're constantly on edge, ready to hit out and blame everything and everyone around you. These feelings spill over and effect your whole family life.

If you ticked numbers 11 or 12, 'You're so anxious' may be your style.
You love your children and want desperately to do your best but have no confidence in your ability to do so.

If you ticked numbers 13 or 14, 'Do it for me' may be your style.
There were many things you wanted to do when you were young that somehow never happened, so now you put immense pressure on your own children to live their lives for you.

If you ticked numbers 15 or 16, 'Good Enough' may be your style.
Not perfect, not saintly but comfortable, confident and loving. Good Enough parents can have moments of being any of the above. But the key to their families is listening and discussing.

Most of us parent with a mixture of those styles, mixing and matching day by day, so you may have found yourself recognizing more than a few of the things you say or think. But none of these styles are set in stone. This book, after all, is about recognizing how you can access support and ideas to do your best as a parent. We don't want to try for perfection – there is no such thing as a Perfect Parent. But if you use some of the parenting tips that follow, the chances are you can be a Good Enough parent – and that's enough.

Looking after yourself

You can't love your child and support them if you don't love and support yourself. Lack of self-belief and self-esteem are your biggest enemies, and feeling a failure and under siege can hamper your efforts to care for all of you. It's really important that you recognize that you need and deserve care, too. So make a point of giving yourself some time off and a treat every now and then and take this advice to heart:

- Be gentle with yourself.
- Remind yourself you are not a magician. You can't work miracles.
- Recognize that other people's problems are their property and responsibility, not yours. You can't fix everything, nor should you try.
- Give support, encouragement and praise. Learn to accept it in return.
- Change your routines often and your tasks when you can.

- Learn to recognize the difference between complaining that offloads and makes you feel better, and complaining that just reinforces stress.
- Focus on one good thing that happens every day.
- Schedule 'you time' periods at least twice a week when you can be calm and at peace and where no one interrupts you.
- Say 'I choose' rather than 'I should' or 'I ought to' or 'I have to' or 'I must'.
- Say 'I won't' rather than 'I can't'.
- Say *no* sometimes – you can't do everything. If you never say *no*, what is your *yes* worth?
- Being aloof, distant or indifferent is far more hurtful and harmful than admitting you can't cope.
- Give yourself permission to have fun – often!

'ACT' rather than react

There is another important reason you should look to yourself first. In any interaction there are two influences – you and the other person. We often feel when children play up that the row is all about them and their behaviour – they're 'behaving badly' and they need to be sorted out.

In fact, what you bring to the interface is just as important – sometimes more so. If you come home angry and upset and the first thing you see is a dirty plate and an open biscuit tin left on the kitchen table and you shout at your child about it, the situation can soon escalate into a row. You may accuse them of being messy, they may come back saying you're overreacting and soon you're at loggerheads. You may say the fault was the child's for leaving a mess, the child may say it was because you didn't give them a chance. You're both at an impasse.

Adult's feelings and needs

Whenever you're in a situation that looks to be spiralling out of control, you need to stop and ask yourself *'What's going on for me? How am I feeling? What do I need to happen?'*

You might initially answer 'Well, I'm annoyed at what the other person has done. I need them to do what I want.' In other words, it was their fault for leaving a mess and you had every right to blow up at them. Is that the whole story? Could the whole answer not be 'I've had a bad day. My boss was demanding, I made some mistakes, the bus was crowded and I felt ready to blow. I need the people at work as well as at home to make my life easier. And I just needed a few minutes to calm down.' Your state of mind contributed to the eventual argument. You couldn't change what was going on elsewhere in your life, so you had a go at your child in an attempt to make them knuckle under and help you feel good. You could call it 'kicking the cat' or letting off steam at one person because of your anger at another.

Child's feelings and needs

Then, ask yourself 'What's going on for my child? How are they feeling? What do they need to happen?'

You might initially answer 'They're lazy and selfish. They shouted back at me because I was in the right and they were in the wrong.' Is that the whole story? Could the whole answer not be 'If I'd asked, maybe they had a bad day too and were just waiting to ask for some support when I came in and shouted. Perhaps if I'd just reminded them, they would have cleaned up at once.'

The toolkit

If you stopped and thought this through, you could then use the skills you have – or will soon have – to find out how you and your child could co-operate and fulfil both of your needs in this situation. In this case, your need for some order, your child's need for a snack and a bit of sympathy and both your needs for reassurance. The skills you do have and will soon enhance are your toolkit – various tips and strategies you have for managing your family as best you can. Add that up: the Adult's feelings and needs; the Child's feelings and needs; and the Toolkit. It spells **ACT**.

A very useful motto is: '**ACT**, don't react'. Instead of reacting to your child's behaviour at once, stop and think it through.

Think:

Adult: *What's going on for me. How am I feeling? What do I need to happen? Why?*

Child: *What's going on for my child. How are they feeling? What do they need to happen? Why?*

Tools: *What can I say or do to help both of us get what we need?*

Acting instead of reacting can help in many ways. It encourages you to recognize that what is happening in other areas of your and your child's life can have an effect on what goes on between you. It helps you see that how you behave has as much to do with the situation as how they behave. It helps you to understand that emotions about other issues can intrude in all sorts of places. And it helps you begin to recognize that there are things you can do to get control.

Case study – Sally's story

It just seemed that Paul lurched from one disaster to another. He argued with me non-stop and refused to talk to his older brother. He got into fights at school and was always on report and in detention. And I was having such a bad time at work – trying to manage and be professional while I was forever getting calls from the school. Oh – and I'd just got a promotion so I was struggling to justify it and feeling really, really out of control, what with their father having left and all. I felt Paul was being so lazy and stupid and downright obstructive to me – I didn't need this. Then a friend of mine came back to my house from work – we were going out together to some do or other. And she saw the usual evening rows and I thought she'd be sympathetic and tell me I had such a rough time of it. But she didn't. She didn't exactly launch into me but she sat me down over a glass of wine and told me how she saw it. And she said as far as she could see, I was the one who went in all bad tempered and spoiling for a fight. She said maybe I was the one who needed to look to how I was feeling and how I was coping, and how I was behaving. Maybe if I changed my approach, so could he. I can't tell you how furious I was! We didn't speak for a week. But we made up because it made me think and I realized she had a point. So I got a couple of parenting books and read through and I tried some new ways of doing it. And I couldn't believe it – it made such a difference. A big difference. I changed, and he changed. And I felt so much better and so did he.

Positive parenting

When you've suffered losses in a family and are under pressure, it's very easy to get into a negative state of mind – to continually find yourself thinking 'I can't cope' and to be saying 'I'm at the end of my tether.' Children will pick this up and start saying 'I can't do that' or 'I'm not good enough to manage this.' Worst of all, all of you may begin to believe 'I'm not good enough for anything better – things always go wrong for me.' Sadly, negative views are a self-fulfilling prophecy. Talk yourself into being pessimistic and you'll never look for the upside. Instead of striving to do better, you'll depress yourself into doing worse.

For yourself and for your children it's important to look for the positive in everything. Instead of saying 'I can't', look for the ways you can. When your children claim they can't, look for ways to encourage and enthuse them into managing.

Being positive means opting for positive parenting. Instead of telling your child off when you're upset or they do something you don't like, praise them when you're happy and they do something you do like. It's a far more effective parenting style. Children want to please you. If you can encourage, praise and tell them how much you care you'll find they respond far better than they might to criticism and punishment. Praise what you like and show that you love them, with hugs, kisses and thanks, and they have every incentive to repeat it, to get the positive attention you are offering. When the only time they get a reaction from you is to tell them off, they'll keep doing the things you don't like because being told off is better than being ignored.

Listening to your children

Listening may seem like a simple matter but, in fact, effective listening is an art and a skill and one you need to acquire and practise to get the best out of yourself and your family. When you think about it, you do know what works in listening and what does not. Having someone pay attention, having someone show they care and understand what you are saying is effective listening. When the other person isn't paying attention, jumps in with quick fixes, tells you it's your fault or tries to brush off your concerns, they are not listening constructively.

What makes the difference are the listening skills we've talked about earlier (p. 9). Listening skills are when the other person shows they're really hearing what you're saying and want to understand and help without taking over. It doesn't mean they have to agree. It does mean what they say and what they do shows you they care about you.

Using the key qualities of active and reflective listening can help in any exchange, whether it's a child telling you about losing a pen, or a friend breaking the news that their marriage has broken up.

Care for, trust and accept the other person and their feelings and make efforts to understand.

Children need to know you respect them and have a belief that they will live up to your expectations. They need to know that while you may not be pleased with their behaviour you are pleased with them. They need you to ask the questions and listen to the answers so you see their point of view.

But don't sort it out for them.

Rushing in and 'fixing' problems for children means they never have the opportunity to sort them out for themselves. Instead, for instance, of always being the one to referee sibling arguments, try first stating the problem: 'I see two children and one toy they both want.' Or: 'You want to watch different programmes on TV.' Then tell them: 'I have confidence that you will work it out yourselves. Come and tell me in five minutes what you have decided.' You will be pleasantly surprised how often, given the chance, that children come up with equable, fair agreements.

Concentrate on this person and this problem, NOW. Listen attentively and give attention to what your children are saying.

Sometimes you have to respond to the question or the remark by dropping everything and paying attention. The evening meal, the ironing, your favourite TV show can wait; often your child cannot. It's not that the particular problem is so vital, it's that when told enough times 'I have more important things to do than listen to you', a child will simply stop coming to you with their worries. Sometimes you have to give them full attention but with your eye elsewhere. Children will often choose the moments you aren't looking them eye to eye to bring up really important issues – when you're driving, washing up, making a meal. You need to cultivate the ability to be giving them your full awareness while not putting them under a spotlight.

Use your body to show you're paying attention.

Leaning forward, turning towards them, having your arms and legs uncrossed all say 'I'm listening and I'm open to what you are saying.' Even when they've chosen a moment when you can't turn to them, you can show them your attention is on them, by listening and making it clear you are doing so.

Ask open questions.

A closed question is one that stops you dead either because the only answer you can give is 'Yes', 'No' or a short, factual reply, or one that says you have already made your mind up about the answer, or a rhetorical question. Examples include:

- What sort of time of you call this?
- You're not going out in that?
- Did you have a good time today?
- Are you alright?

In contrast, try asking each of these as open questions:

- You said you'd be back at 10 and I was really worried. Would you tell me why you came in later than we agreed?
- Wow – that T-shirt seems a bit skimpy. I'd be worried that someone might hassle you if you went out in that. What do you think?
- You look as if you had a good time. Tell me about it.
- You don't look very well. Tell me how you're feeling.

Check out what's been said.

When someone is telling you something, it's always useful to check out what they're saying as you go along. Checking out has two functions. It lets the other person know you're listening and trying to understand. And it gives you the chance to know you are on the right track, and them the chance to correct you if you've misunderstood. Say: 'Have I got this right, you feel...', 'You're saying...', 'It sounds as if ...'.

Acknowledge feelings.

When a child feels upset, angry, jealous or rejected it often helps simply to hear someone say 'You're feeling furious about that, aren't you?' You don't need to offer a solution or try to improve or soften the situation. You just have to say 'This is what you're feeling and I hear it' for them to feel better. Sometimes, just acknowledging the feelings and needs is enough. At other times the person who is talking may want to think about how they are going to sort out the problem. Be guided by them – our role as listener is to offer care and understanding, not come up with a solution.

Identify needs.

What you can then do is identify the need underneath the feeling. If someone feels jealous they may need their requirement for affection or time met by you. If they feel angry they may need to know you understand why. Acknowledge the feeling, and then see if you can identify what need it shows.

What's the need?
It is probably for comfort, security, reassurance, approval.

What might a child be feeling if their needs aren't being met?
They may be feeling scared, angry, jealous, rejected.

What might they be saying?
'I hate you!', 'I wish Dad was still here!', 'Why can't we be like other families?'

What might their behaviour be?
Crying, slamming doors, refusing to sleep, fighting.

So when you get bad behaviour – slamming doors, tears and tantrums – listen also to the words. When you've heard the words, think about what the child may actually be feeling under all that. Then, consider what the needs that are not being met may be. Try playing back the needs to them, by tapping into the words. 'It sounds as if you're upset about your dad not being here. Can we talk about it?'

Move them on.

Once you have acknowledged the feelings and identified the need, the next step is to move the person on. This isn't the same as fixing it for them – you aren't implementing a solution all on your own. You're suggesting solutions you might like and asking them for those they might like, and ones that both of you can live with. The key is to help your child fix their own problems, not do it for them. Ask yourself, what are the possible solutions?

- Can you find a solution that gives everyone some of what they want?
- What helps and what hinders this solution?
- How could any obstacles be overcome?

Your AIM when you are listening is to:

- **A**cknowledge feelings – 'I can see you're angry.'
- **I**dentify needs – 'You wanted to be able to stay out late with your friends.'
- **M**ove on – 'What can we do to satisfy both of us?'

Essential points

- If you want to look after your children you first have to look after yourself.
- ACT, don't react; pay attention to the Adult's feelings and needs, the Child's feelings and needs and then look to your Toolkit of strategies.
- Listen and talk with your children, using good communication skills, to make sure you understand each other.

Case study

Jumoke was having trouble in school and her mother, Jo, was frantic because every time she tried to help it ended in arguments. Jo started going to a parenting workshop and learnt about reflective listening. Here's what Jumoke had to say about what happened next: 'I was having trouble at school, right, and every time I tried to talk with Mum about it, it was like she tried to tell me what to do, or just wasn't there – she wasn't listening. Or she'd just ask me what I was doing wrong to be getting such hassle. She started going to these classes and I thought they were a load of rubbish. But then I noticed something. See, I came home having had a load of grief and I didn't want to talk to her in case I got even more, but I said something. And she stopped what she was doing and sat down and just said 'Uhuh?' So I told her what had happened and by the end of it, we were working it out and I went back to school next day and really sorted it out. But when I looked back, Mum hadn't told me what to do and she hadn't told me off and she hadn't even said much. But it was like she was really listening and had really helped. And she's been like that since – I'm not sure how she does it but it feels good. Maybe those parent classes aren't such rubbish after all.'

Next time your child needs to talk to you, try this:

- Listen uncritically, trusting them, accepting how they say they feel and make efforts to understand what they are saying and how they are feeling. Say 'I'm listening – tell me about it.'
- Resist the urge to jump in with solutions – you're there to be a sounding board, not a fixer. Say 'That sounds difficult. What do you think?'
- Concentrate on them – you can keep washing up if you feel they would shy off an eye-to-eye confrontation, but give your full attention. Say 'Uh-huh?'
- Use your body to show you are paying attention – turn towards them, don't cross your arms. Say...nothing! But show you're concentrating on them.
- Ask open questions. Say 'Tell me about your day.'
- Check out what's being said. Say 'Have I got this right? You're saying...'
- Acknowledge feelings. Say 'I can see you feel...'
- Identify needs. Say 'It sounds to me as if...'
- Move them on. Say 'So what do you want to do about this?'

Negotiating skills

Negotiation means coming to an agreement with everyone happy with what's been decided. It might seem to take a bit longer than simply putting your foot down, but in the long run it's quicker, works better and leaves everyone happy.

How do you negotiate?
- Someone makes a request.
- You all gather information about what they and you want.
- You discuss it.
- You come to mutual understanding and agreement.

What helps and what gets in the way of negotiation?
It holds you back if you:

- think you know what your child should do, and are sure you're right
- make judgments about your child or what they want
- let your own feelings, of fear or anger or envy, get in the way.

It helps if you:

- listen without interrupting
- give your child your full attention
- really want to understand what your child is feeling and needing, and let them know that
- keep checking out that you understand what is wanted and what is going on.

Labelling children works against you

You label a child when you say what you think they are. 'You're lazy', 'You're messy', 'You're selfish'.

There are two big problems with this. The first is that none of these tell the child exactly what they're doing that so upsets you. It gives them no clue as to what you don't like and what you'd prefer for them to be doing. They can't change because they don't know what to change.

The second problem is that by telling a child what they **are** you make the clear statement that they cannot change – this, after all, is what they **are**. Children may be confused. Even if they do know exactly what is so upsetting you they still have no incentive to alter their ways because, after all, they are stuck with being like that. That's what they **are**.

When you're upset it works better to tell your children what is bothering you than blaming them. And it opens up a whole new ball game when, instead of labelling the child you identify the behaviour. You identify what they **do**, not what they **are**.

Instead of: 'You're lazy.'

Try: 'It upsets me when you sit down when I'm doing all the work. I'd like you to help me, please.'

Instead of: 'You're so messy.'

Try: 'You left all your clothes on the floor. Tidy them up, please.'

Instead of: 'You're selfish.'

Try: 'You got yourself a snack and left the cat hungry. Feed her first, please.'

You'll find labelling the behaviour instead of labelling the child takes some of the heat out of the situation and lets them change. You can always change what you do, but not what you are.

How to talk so children will listen

The way we talk has a huge effect on the people we are talking to. Depending on the words we use, our tone of voice and our body language (the way we stand, use our hands, look or don't look at the other person) the other person may experience blame, judgement, criticism or feel bullied or ignored. Using the language of blame and judgement damages our relationships with other people. And it means neither of us get what we want from the situation.

Getting the point across

When we talk, we want:

- to be clear about how we're feeling and what we need
- to show the other person that we care about them and their needs
- to give them a reason to help us to get what we need
- to bring us together rather than drive us apart.

People will feel more like doing what we want if they:

- understand how we feel and why something is important to us
- hear clear 'I' messages rather than blaming 'you' messages
- are given a choice or hear requests rather than demands
- know we have listened to them and understood how they are feeling and what they need.

What is meant by 'I' messages and 'you' messages

Were you told at school that 'I' doesn't get'? Most of us grow up thinking it sounds selfish or arrogant to say 'I' so we get in the habit of saying 'Everyone' or 'You'. But when we're talking with the people who matter, this gets in the way of real communication. If you tell a child 'You make me angry' or 'Look what you made me do!', you often find yourself in an argument. They hear judgement and blame, which hurts, so they fight back. They didn't mean to make you angry or for you to drop and break a cup, so why blame them for it? 'I' statements can help.

When you're finding it difficult to talk things through, it might be because of the way you're phrasing it. It could help to use an 'I' statement. 'I' statements are all about being able to say what 'I feel', 'I want' and what 'I need'. They help the person speaking, and the person being spoken to, be clear about what is really going on.

When you use an 'I' statement, you can:

- be aware of your own feelings about what you want
- stand up and be counted about your feelings and needs
- help other people to understand what you are saying
- be clear, honest and direct
- make your point without blaming, criticizing or judging other people.

When you're upset you sometimes blame the other person for what has happened. 'Look what you made me do' or 'You make me so angry!' Or you try to avoid taking responsibility for angry or critical remarks by saying they belong to someone else: 'Everyone thinks it's your fault.'

These are 'You' statements and they seldom give the other person a chance to understand what you're upset about, how you feel or why, or give them an opportunity to make any changes. 'You' statements may be a way of not being overwhelmed by anger or despair. Instead of 'owning' feelings, you hold them at arms length: 'One feels like that, doesn't one?' 'That's how you do it, don't you?'

Using an 'I' statement respects the other person and their point of view. It helps you say what you feel and want but avoids making the other person feel like the problem. This makes it far easier for them to come up with a solution, take responsibility and act positively.

It can take some time to get into the habit of using 'I' statements, which isn't surprising. Most of us have had a lifetime of being told it's selfish or big-headed to say 'I'. But the more you use them, the more you'll find they work and help you and the other person feel good about the exchange.

An 'I' statement:

- describes the behaviour I'm finding difficult
- says the effect it has on me
- tells the other person how I feel about it
- invites them to join me in finding a solution.

A good way to get this across is to:

- give a clear, specific, direct and factual description of what is happening: 'When…'
- express your feelings: 'I feel…'
- explain why you feel that way: 'Because…'
- state what you would like to happen: 'I would like'… or invite discussion 'What can we do about it?'

Understanding bad behaviour

Feelings can be frightening. You love your child but you may also feel angry with them, and sad, lost and resentful. Your child may have strong emotions, too, of fear, rage and misery. Parents often want to protect their children from anything that could hurt. You sometimes try to deny or push bad feelings away, thinking that if you pretend everything is okay, it will be. But far from making these feelings go away, trying to hide or reject them can make them worse. It's often important to face up to emotions and talk them through, and to accept that your kids can have them too.

Kids have minds of their own. They have tastes and opinions, friends and views that are all their own, that may be different from yours. It can be a shock to realize your little boy or girl, at a surprisingly young age, is separate and different from you. You might want to fight this, to rein them in and keep control. It's so much more fun to respect their differences and enjoy them. It's also far more effective to deal with bad behaviour by understanding what it might be about rather than just seeking to control it or make it go away.

To fully understand bad behaviour, you first need to look at what children need (see p. 56). Teenagers need exactly the same as they always have, with one proviso. Part of being a teenager is pulling away from you and learning how to be themselves. This can mean there are times when they don't want to listen to you, talk with you or even be with you.

The key is to make sure the channels of communication remain open, to go on talking and to keep listening. Children of all ages need to know we care about them, are interested in them and are on their side. Even if we disagree, it's the issue we are at odds about, not them.

What to do if it seems you always argue, never talk

Constant fights can feel like being on a roundabout. Every comment and response seems to be like a script you repeat again and again as you go round and round. How do you stop it? One of you has to, it might as well be you.

How to stop a 'roundabout'

Stop pushing!

Roundabouts don't go round on their own. You start them up and keep them going by reacting. Remember the 'ACT don't react' motto? Break the pattern and refuse to get wound up. Ignore behaviour that irritates you. Just let it go.

Jump off!

- Make an effort to change the way you talk, using 'I' statements and other listening and talking skills.
- If you want to talk about something upsetting or sensitive, bring it up yourself when you're calm and ready instead of reacting angrily to something the child says or does.
- Chat with your child. Talk about something that interests you and draw them in. Encourage them to talk about things that interest them.
- Use listening skills to show an interest without asking too many questions.
- Be there when they are at home.
- Tell them the things you like about them.
- Remind them you care without words: with a hand on the shoulder, a cup of tea, anything that just says 'I am here and I care about you.'

Use your weight as a brake

Slow down the roundabout of arguments by refusing to play that game anymore. Don't forget, you are the adult and so older and wiser. The bottom line is that you're the grown up and you're in charge. Yes, you'll listen, respect and negotiate. But you will put the boundaries in place, and you will maintain them. If you believe in yourself, your teenager will believe in you. If they think you believe in them, they will gradually start to believe in themselves.

Don't expect an immediate response

After all, that roundabout is still going round. It will take a while for the penny to drop – that you have stopped pushing.

Doesn't giving in all the time spoil them?

Giving children what they need isn't the same as giving in, or the same as:

- always putting them first – you have needs, too
- doing everything for them or giving them everything they want – sometimes they need to wait, or make some effort, or accept they can't have what they choose
- not having boundaries. What children sometimes need is for you to say no, and mean it.

You can't protect your children from all unhappiness or problems and it wouldn't help them if you could. Being able to enjoy the ups and get through the downs will help them make the most of life, as a child and as an adult. But we do know that spending time with children and paying attention to them makes your life, and theirs, easier and happier. As far as a child is concerned, any attention is better than none. If no one listens or talks or plays or hugs, they'll act up until someone shouts or hits.

You can reinforce good behaviour by making time with *small* children to:

- read to and with them
- sing songs and nursery rhymes
- paint and draw
- play with letters and numbers
- visit libraries, museums and other places
- create regular opportunities to meet and play with other children.

You can reinforce good behaviour by making time with *school age* children to:

- read to and with them
- show an interest in what they are doing – in home, outside home, in school
- emphasize the importance of homework
- visit libraries, museums and other places
- create regular opportunities to make and reinforce social networks with other children
- attend plays, concerts, sports events etc.

You can reinforce good behaviour by making time with *teenagers* to:

- discuss books, TV programmes and films with them
- share meals with them
- ask for and respect their opinions
- show an interest in what they are doing – at home, outside home, at school or college
- encourage them to have friends and to bring them home.

Why do children behave badly?

Bad behaviour is always about something. Children don't behave badly just because they are naughty, they misbehave for reasons. However, children often find it hard to understand or explain their feelings. So, they tend to 'act them out'. So called 'bad behaviour' is often the only way they can express their emotions and reactions. If children 'defy' you, it's better to dive under the behaviour to understand what's going on than get into a head-to-head fight. All behaviour is a way of getting what you need. Bad behaviour is actually a way of trying to show bad feelings. When we can understand what our children need and why they do what they do, we can help them help us.

Would discipline help?

When someone says 'discipline' most of us think about punishment. It's about keeping our children in line and doing the right thing. But the original meaning of the word is 'to teach'. Discipline is something we do to help children learn. And the best way to get children to behave in ways that please us is to help them understand what they actually want and need, and to see how they can get those needs met in ways that don't upset other people. Respond to the underlying need rather than the 'bad behaviour' and the child's reason for behaving that way melts away. One thing children lose when families break up is control. It wasn't their choice for their parents to separate and for one parent to be out of touch. What is happening around them can make them feel utterly powerless. This can lead to their trying to gain some control and exercise some choice in their lives, often with drastic and confusing effect. Bad behaviour can be a way of saying 'I can't get what I really want so I'll try and get something.'

To help children behave better, as already mentioned, you may need to start with yourself. When concentrating on the children and how they behave, you may be ignoring the fact that you too can be feeling angry, left out and rejected. You may be showing this through shouting, being depressed and not listening to them. Once you can deal with your own emotions and reactions you can turn to your children and deal with theirs. **The best way of 'disciplining' children is often to set out to help, not punish them.** After all, half the time if you punish a child for acting up in a single family, what you are actually doing is punishing them for being sad at what has happened to them and trying to let you know about it. Where's the justice in that?

It may not seem like it sometimes, but children want to please their parents and win their approval. When they feel you have understood what they need, and can understand you in turn, they have the incentive to change. If you can tell them clearly what you want and why, and respect and listen to them, you'll get a better result than simply coming down hard on them.

Why children show their feelings in actions

The acting out that so often leads to debates about discipline is because children and young people may find it hard to tell you how they feel about the changes and losses they have suffered. Instead, they are likely to show their feelings by what they do. They often believe the change or loss is somehow their fault, which can add to their confusion and make it harder for them to talk about their feelings. Children may show distress by:

- acting younger than their age
- wetting the bed
- throwing tantrums
- forgetting skills they've learned
- becoming clingy and fretful
- refusing food, being picky or eating too much
- having difficulty sleeping or in waking up.

Teenagers may:

- refuse to talk
- be angry
- experiment with drugs, drink, early sex.

Understanding what is underneath the behaviour

It's not discipline in the form of punishment or control that children need when they behave badly in a single family situation. What is underneath their behaviour is often a need for attention, acceptance, appreciation, and some independence. They are often fighting to get these when they act up. We can help them by:

- talking openly about the change or loss that has lead to their being in a single family
- helping them to show their feelings
- sharing our own feelings with them
- telling them it's okay to feel bad
- asking their opinions
- giving them plenty of time and attention
- making sure some things don't change
- helping them keep in touch with people, places, things that matter to them
- helping them remember people, places, things that matter through photos, letters, drawings, objects
- keeping them busy doing things they enjoy
- giving them love, reassurance, support
- cutting them some slack and accepting that they will act up.

Essential points

- Don't label children – describe the behaviour you don't like so they can understand what you'd like them to change.
- Using 'I' statements rather than 'You' statements helps people to understand your feelings.
- Bad behaviour is a way of trying to get needs met. When children feel bad they often 'act out' their emotions with their behaviour.

From the postbag

Dealing with my teenagers is like trying to herd cats. If one gets what he wants, the others complain. If I try to put my foot down, one or two or all three of them will have some reason why it shouldn't apply to them. They're always coming to me with requests and questions and it feels as if I say the same thing, again and again. I point out it's really hard managing on my own and they are sympathetic, don't get me wrong. They're good boys and really lovely people. It's just that it feels as if I'm trying to do so much and I can't keep up.

It sounds as if you'd benefit from two strategies. One is giving them far more responsibility themselves. Especially with teenagers, and especially in a single parent household, it can help to hand over some responsibility and tell them to manage it. The other is for you to institute a family discussion once a week and tell them to be there or lose out – you won't repeat things and you won't debate things that have come up there and been agreed by who's at the discussion. It's an excellent way of getting agreements and consensus, on hearing everyone's point of view and needs and getting them to balance them out. Put your foot down on this one thing – that you're going to have them – and then you won't have to fight again. Good luck!

Breaking the cycle and sorting difficulties

One good way of breaking the cycle and sorting any bad behaviour you are experiencing is by using family discussions to find out what people want and how they can have it.

We sometimes use family discussions as a way of telling children what we have decided to do. They're a good way of getting everyone together and being clear about what the adults have determined. But family discussions can be even more effective – and fun – if they become a time and place where everyone has a say. Where, in effect, you work together rather than have adults simply laying down the law.

If young people are given as much space and respect to have their say as adults, the result may be that they get some of what they want and you get less of what you would choose. But when young people have an input into decision making and are heard, they usually 'buy in' to what has been decided, being far more cooperative than when it is imposed. In the long run that means less work and more fun. A family parliament is an ideal way, not just of making agreements that stick and keeping in touch, but also of pulling everyone together. In a single family, it really helps to make time and space for regular family discussions. There are three main rules to make a family discussion work.

1 Make sure everyone gets their say

Everyone, from oldest to youngest, is to have an equal turn to speak and to be heard. You might like to go around the table letting each person say one thing, to start. Then, take turns to add to the discussion. You can use an object handed round to signify whose turn it is to speak – an ornament, a kitchen implement such as a spoon or a pencil. Ask everyone to keep the rule about only talking when they have had it handed to them, and handing it on when finished. It helps to appoint one person to act as the 'facilitator' for a family discussion, and to have each member of the group take it in turn to play this role. The facilitator ensures that everyone takes it in turns to speak and not interrupt.

2 Help everyone to 'own' what they say

The most important rule is that everyone has to 'own' what they say. That means, everything you put forward has to be your own thoughts and feelings and you should acknowledge them as such, saying 'I think' or 'I feel'. No one can say 'So-and-so says' or 'Everyone knows' or talk about what other people intend or what you think they think. You can talk about how other people's behaviour affects you, by saying 'When you do such-and-such, I feel...' but the aim is to put across your point of view, not to criticize or attack other people. Remember, the key is confronting problems, not people.

3 Come to a consensus

The eventual aim of your discussion is to find a space where everyone feels they have been heard and appreciated, and have heard and appreciated everyone else's point of view. There should be no winners or losers, but an all-round agreement on the outcome. To that end, no one is to be shouted down for what they say. Discuss the points rather than arguing with the person. Set aside time for the discussion and allow everyone a chance to speak, as many times as they like.

Ask for help but trust yourself

As a parent, you love and want to do what's best for your child. It's worthwhile asking for and getting help from professionals and friends. But you are the best expert on your own family. Trust yourself if you think anything is wrong or if you think the advice you've been given won't work for you. You can't be a perfect parent, no one can be perfect. The best any parent can aim at is being Good Enough and if you love and value your child and tell them so, you're doing the best anyone can do. Ask for their input and always respect their needs and opinions, and listen to what they have to say. But in the end, you're the adult. This isn't a democracy, it's a benevolent dictatorship. You're the one who enforces the rules and holds the boundaries. And you have the skills to do so.

Summary

- Recognizing your parenting style, and making changes if necessary, can be a helpful parenting strategy.
- You cannot care for others effectively unless you look after yourself first.
- Your actions and reactions have a considerable effect on your child. Use the ACT technique to help you understand what is going on and communicate with them.
- Effective listening and effective talking are essential for good communication. They are both skills that have to be learned and practised.
- Bad behaviour is always about trying to get needs met. Dive beneath the behaviour to understand the message and deal with that, not the behaviour itself. Once the needs are met the behaviour usually resolves.
- Identifying what your child really needs, and what you need yourself, puts you well on the way to becoming a Good Enough parent.

06

home alone

In this chapter you will learn:
- how new starts and makeovers can help
- how to begin the way you intend to continue
- about agreeing a set of family rules
- how to pick your battles
- about the importance of family chores
- how to make your home a safe foundation for your family.

Making the most of being alone

There are losses in becoming a single parent – the loss of the other adult, the loss of a relationship, the loss of your hopes and dreams about bringing up your family together, the loss of someone to talk to and share adult fun with. But there are also certain freedoms and gains. You can do as you like – eat biscuits in bed, sit up late watching the films you choose, maybe start eating healthily without a partner sabotaging you by saying they like you how you are and where are the crisps? You can build up a closer relationship with your children, and have time with them without it seeming a choice between them and a partner. And you can decide what is right for you and them – a distinct plus if parenting styles were a point of contention before you became a single parent. There may be a welcome freedom from conflict along with an increase in your self-esteem.

Top tip

If you're finding it hard being a single parent, try this tip. Every day, think of one positive thing – only one – about being a parent on your own. Add a new one every day. It can be a little, trivial matter or something really significant. Write them down and when you're feeling despondent, check back on the growing list.

Whatever has happened, and whether you're still reeling from separation or deciding to take stock after a period of being a single parent, affirming what you've got and beginning a new era is important. Whether you are moving home, or adjusting your old one to your partner no longer being there, a significant step towards claiming your life and the life of your children for yourselves would be to set out to make this a home that exactly suits you. Everyone has fantasies of what would make their perfect home. What usually holds us back is money, inertia and disagreements with the other adult over what we'd like. What would suit you perfectly often doesn't ring your partner's bells. If you only have yourself and your children to please, you're a big step towards getting what you want. You may still not have the money but you don't have the other person to stop you – all you now need to do is fight the tendency to inaction.

How to set up your own home

The first step, of course, is recognizing you can do this. It's your home and your right. Whatever the situation before now, it's changed. You're in charge.

If you're staying put

Plan a change-around with your kids. Ideas storm what you'd all like. These suggestions might start you off:

- Move the furniture around. It's amazing how different a home can look and feel simply by rearranging the sofas and chairs, and how much it says 'This is a new beginning.' People do tend to have 'their own' seat in places in the home and if everything stays as it is, the family can feel it's someone else's chair they're trespassing in, and notice that there is an absence. Change it around and there is no longer someone gone – there's more room for you. And everyone can claim areas as their own. Give some thought to how you could use rooms and plan accordingly.

- Consider an 'all change' in who has what room. Think about sizes of rooms, where they are in the house and how they are used. Mull over whether with one less person in the house you might propose something different. You may, for instance, still assume you'd have the master bedroom. Putting two younger children or a teenager in it to use as a playroom or bed-sitting room and your having a smaller room and first claim on the living room might be more practical.

- Redecorate, allowing each person to choose the colour and decoration in their own room and arrive at a consensus (as the grown up, you're allowed the veto) in main rooms. DIY and use charity shops or material exchanges to cut down on costs.

If you're moving

House hunt with your children and plan the eventual layout with them.

- Give some thought to how you could use rooms and plan accordingly.

- Think about size of rooms, where they are in the house and how they are used and consider carefully who has what room – as when staying put, giving the largest bedroom to two younger children or a teenager to use as a bed-sitting room and your having a smaller room and first claim on the living room may be the best use of space.

- When you decorate, allow each person to choose the colour and decoration in their own room and arrive at a consensus (as the grown up, you're allowed the veto) in main rooms. DIY and use charity shops or material exchanges to cut down on costs.

How to move on while keeping links with the past

Whether it's a new home or an old one re-made, you need to balance certain elements you want with those your children need. You may very well desire a complete makeover, clearing out things that remind you of a home before you were a single parent – pictures and ornaments, but most of all photographs. To you, that might spell a fresh start and a breath of fresh air. To your children, however, it could mean a total crumbling of foundations. They need some reminders of the past to link them with who they are, and they may need some familiarity to give them security. However much they may rub a raw spot with you, your children will need you to encourage them to keep and display photographs, to have pictures, ornaments and toys that have always been there to reassure them that some things do not leave them, abandon them or reject them. You may need to negotiate with them:

- what remains
- whether items that have been on public display may now be put elsewhere
- that what they have in their rooms is their own and only their own choice.

Making over yourself

As well as rearranging the home, give some thought to rearranging yourself, your habits and your life. If you're going to move on you may need to help yourself by doing something – quiet or downright dramatic – to signal to yourself and everyone else that the old stops here and the new begins. Start by:

- Having a makeover. It's a classic ploy when relationships change to have a new hair cut, new grooming and new styles. However clichéd it feels, it really does work.

- Going through your wardrobe. Divide everything into three piles – stuff you wear all the time, stuff you've worn in the last year, stuff you haven't worn for a year. Give the last to a charity shop, review the second again, and have a long look at the first.
- Visiting your local leisure centre or college and booking a class – learn Italian, creative writing, painting. Fulfil a long-held ambition or do it simply to meet new people.
- Taking some exercise. Go for a walk, a run, a cycle or join a gym. Make a date to do that at least twice a week from now on.

You might then like to ideas storm, with a friend or family member if it would help, changes you could make in your life. Some suggestions may be:

- training, to improve your earning power
- joining a class to learn something new, for the fun of it
- counselling, to settle any lingering regrets or to explore changes you'd like to make that might help you.

Sometimes a radical overhaul is needed in order for you to see what assumptions you may be making about your capabilities and competencies. A counsellor could help you confront these. You may have always thought you needed someone to be by your side to look after you, and now is the time to realize you can manage on your own. And if that supposition can be overturned, what other assumptions about what you can and can't do might be wrong? Some people seize on a fear they have always had and deal with it, such as learning to climb to confront a fear of heights or taking a course to shake off a fear of flying. Strengthened by realizing they can do things they had always told themselves they could not, many go on to look at getting qualifications they never felt they could achieve and jobs they never felt they'd manage.

Case study

Chris had grown up with animals in the home – cats, a dog, hamsters. When he married Sally, he wanted to get a dog but she said no – they were too much trouble. When they had their first baby, Amy, and he said children benefited from having pets, she disagreed. Chris and Sally divorced when Amy and Saul were ten and seven and when Sally and her new husband decided to move to Australia, the children stayed with Chris. Chris suggested to the children that they overhaul and move the house around, with all of them having different bedrooms and making changes to the decoration and the layout of the ground floor too. They kept most of the ornaments and pictures that had always been there but in different places, and Chris started a wall of pictures in the hall with photos of the whole family – him, the children, Sally and her new husband and their new baby in various combinations. One of the requests the children made was to have a pet, so Chris got two kittens and a dog, with the strict understanding that feeding, play and exercise duties were to be shared. Chris had no illusions that losing their mother and having their family turned upside down was a devastating blow to the children and that they all had a lot to process and deal with. But he did feel that some of the changes they had made meant his children would benefit and handle the situation better.

How to begin the way you intend to continue

Set the tone for the way you are going to manage in the future by doing some things for **yourself**:

- Set your alarm clock and get up to watch the sun rise.
- Think of something that scares the pants off you – and go and do it.
- Pick something you always thought of as a special treat – a bottle of champagne, posh chocolates, a new DVD. Buy it for yourself and enjoy it – you deserve it.
- Call/see/email a friend and have a gossip and a laugh. Discuss only happy things – no 'driving the BMW' (Bitching, Moaning, Whinging).
- Make one new contact today – say 'Hello', smile and chat to someone.
- Let your imagination run riot in planning a holiday away – the holiday of your dreams if you won the lottery.
- Work out what made your dream holiday so special and use those elements to plan a break you could manage.
- Do something that has a result that satisfies you – do the ironing, wash the car, clean the bathroom. Bask in your achievement.
- If you have a cat or dog, give it an hour of your time. Play with string, throw a stick or go for a walk.

- If you don't have a pet, discuss with your children whether to get one.
- Put something living in your living room – a bunch of flowers or a pot-plant.

Then do some things **with and for the family**:

- If you don't already do so, make it a rule to sit down with your family to eat a meal together at least once a day. If you have to, rearrange timetables so that this can happen.
- Choose one night a week and make it games night – find an old-fashioned board game you all like and play it together.
- Go for a Sunday walk together – wrap up warm or get out the wellies and do it whatever the weather.
- Choose to be a family, together. Move all computers into the main rooms/spaces, take televisions out of children's bedrooms and negotiate the hours they can spend online and watching. Watch only programmes people really want rather than having it as wallpaper and settle disagreements about what to watch with discussion, not argument.
- Agree a set of family rules.

Essential points

- It's your home so you can set it up to run and to look the way you like.
- Ideas storm with your children what they and you would like.
- Balance your need to leave the past behind with their need to keep some links.

Family rules

Every family has rules they live by. Sometimes, these have been discussed and everyone knows them. Sometimes, they're sort-of known and sort-of agreed. Often, they do exist but people aren't always sure what they are exactly, and they do change from time to time. The aftermath of becoming a single parent family is a time when children may be feeling confused and unclear about what might be expected of them and what they can expect. Giving them clear boundaries can help deal with the uncertainty. Putting together a set of family rules means you have to discuss them, agree them and learn what they are. Then there's no excuse for not realizing what you should or should not be doing.

Here's a set of family rules one family came up with:

- Take your shoes off at the door.
- Don't throw coats on the floor – hang them up.
- If you have a snack, put plates and mugs in the dishwasher and clean the table.
- Feed the cat before feeding yourself.
- Do your chores with no arguments.
- When you're out your mobile phone must be on.
- Talk with each other instead of shouting at each other.
- No kicking, hitting, shoving, biting, swearing or shouting.
- Be kind, be positive, praise often and always say 'please', 'thank you' and 'well done'.
- If you want someone to hear you, you have to listen to them.
- Help people do better instead of criticizing them to bring them down.
- Have a family talk at least once a week.
- Go out as a family at least once a month.
- Go to bed at agreed times.
- Do homework at the beginning of a night or weekend.
- Pocket money to be given every Friday night.
- Say what time you'll be home and keep to it.

You might find some of these appealing, some not suitable for you. You and your family can doubtless come up with a collection that fits your particular situation and needs.

Discussing family rules is important in any family but it can be particularly helpful in a single parent family. This is because what led you to be on your own may well have left all of you feeling out of control and powerless. On the one hand you may be fiercely protective of your lone family, determined that you're going to do your best and adamant that the fact that the other parent is not there is going to make no difference to your children or yourself. But on the other hand there may well be a sense of loss and of something missing in the heart of the family. When children are feeling rootless and rejected they may act out their feelings, either by challenging you or bickering with their siblings. Coping with that sometimes needs strong boundaries and a stable foundation. Family rules can help you to put those in place.

Encouraging your family to 'buy in' to the rules

By talking the rules through and allowing everyone to have their say, you get two results. One is that everyone should 'buy in' to the rules. If everyone sets them, they had a chance to make them or alter them, and know they should keep them. For every rule that you would like to impose, there should be one the children put forward. So rules can be negative – no swearing, shouting or hitting. But they can also be positive – one night a week must be games night when children can choose a game to play – Monopoly, Cluedo, Scrabble, whatever – and you have to take part. Or that they get ten minutes at the end of the day of uninterrupted time to tell you what they've been doing since breakfast.

Another result of talking through the rules is that setting them helps *you*, as well as young people, think about why they are needed and what might be the effect of having – or not having – them. Sometimes, it helps you realize your priorities. After all, does it really matter if a child's room is untidy? Surely having sensible times for them to come home, or go to bed, are more important. And if you kick up a major fuss over the less important things, you may find it hard to insist on something that really *is* central – you've used up all your arguments and sanctions on something less imperative. Discussing rules allows you to choose your battles. And you'll be surprised how sensible young people can be, given the responsibility and the option.

How to decide your family rules

You set family rules by all getting together around a table with a big sheet of paper and some pens. This is the first stage – you're not looking for perfection or neatness at this point. Appoint someone to be the note taker. And then ideas storm – put down every single idea that comes to mind. Ask 'What family rules do we think we already have? What family rules do we want?' You might also ask 'What problems do we have and how could we do something about them?'

Write down every suggestion. Even if you think them unworkable, silly, or too difficult to manage. The only thing you should exclude might be rules that anyone suggests with the intention of 'getting at' another member of the family. So, 'No coming in and taking my make-up' would not be acceptable. But 'Everyone to ask before using anyone else's belongings' is fair – it applies to all.

Having written everything down, go to the second stage: look at and consider the suggestions. Think about what you all want to achieve. Some of your rules may be about getting on with each other – about being kind and helpful. You might put in a rule about not swearing, hitting, fighting or shouting. Some may be about running the home smoothly – you might have a family rule about always putting lunch boxes back in the kitchen, or hanging coats up when you come in or washing up your own cups. Some may be about big and important things such as teenagers always carrying mobile phones when they're out at night with friends and never getting into a car with a driver who's been drinking.

The third stage is agreeing which rules you will select to be your family rules. You might like to rewrite rules to make them as constructive as possible – that is, use dos rather than don'ts. Be as specific as possible – a vague rule about respecting people is less helpful than saying people should listen to each other, not shout them down, interrupt or call them names. You may find you have some overlapping rules – prune or combine. There may be some suggestions that you don't like, and some the children don't like. Make your case and listen to theirs. Do some 'horse trading' – you'll accept one rule they request if they accept another you champion.

Then, write them out neatly. Agree you will all keep to them – you might like to draw up a contract that says so, and everyone (you included) signs it.

How to draw up a contract and why it's a good idea

It helps to write down exactly what everyone has agreed. Make a precise record, which might include:

- what you've all agreed to do
- how you agree to do it
- when you agree to do it by
- for how long you have agreed to do this.

Everyone should sign the contract. Hang up the family rules and the contract somewhere you can all see them and revisit them regularly – maybe once a week. Are they working? If not, why not? What needs to be changed so they will work?

How to spread the load around the family

Once you have your family rules you may like to look at ways of making sure that running your home and your family is as comfortable and harmonious as possible. One way of doing that is to share out the work a bit. If you believe the business of running the home is an adult-only affair, as a lone parent you have your work cut out as all of it lies on your shoulders. But why do you think that? Involving children in doing chores is important in any family. It's absolutely vital in single parent families.

Essential points

• Family rules are important in any family but can be particularly helpful in a single parent family.

• Once you've agreed family rules, it often helps to agree a contract to manage how you're all keeping to the rules.

• Drawing up a chore chart and fairly distributing household task enables everyone in the home to pull their weight.

Chores

Single parents often shy away from asking their children to do chores. Sometimes it's because you are so protective of your children, feeling they've been through enough so it would be unfair to burden them. Sometimes it's because you fear that getting them to help around the house might suggest you can't manage on your own, and you really don't want anyone thinking that. But all children should do chores, even very young children, for the reasons listed below.

• Children want to help. It's their home too and they know they are equal inhabitants not privileged guests.

• You aren't a slave or a servant, put on earth to look after everyone else. When children do chores, they have a respect for you and appreciate what it takes to keep a home running.

• When everyone pulls their weight it means everyone can have some free time. Having you do it all means that one person is tired and sometimes resentful. Shared responsibility means you have more time to have fun together.

• Sometime soon, children will leave to run their own homes. Leaving comes as more of a shock, and can end in disaster, if they haven't acquired the skills to look after themselves and a recognition of what it takes.

From the postbag

I can't get my family to do chores. I just don't have the time. I know it would lead to endless fights just getting them to do what I ask and if they did do them, they'd do them so badly that I'd just have to follow them round picking up the mess and doing them all over again. It all sounds very nice, but it isn't realistic.

Certainly, if you go into sharing the household tasks with a pessimistic, powerless attitude it's likely to backfire. If you assume they'll do it badly, if you follow on behind doing the things you've asked them to do, children have no incentive to fulfil their responsibilities. So let's see how you can turn this around. Firstly, stop thinking of it as something you're getting or asking them to do. What will happen is that all of you will have a discussion about what it takes to keep a home running, and the children are going to recognize that you have enough on your plate and can't do it all. They are going to see that if they live here and expect their clothes to be cleaned and food to be put on the table, some sharing out of chores needs to be done. It's not an argument or a request – it's a recognition of realities. When you simply put it that this will be done – full stop, no argument... kids usually fall in. Especially if they understand how much you need their help and how much it will mean that they can be relied on.

Secondly, start trusting them. Yes, it may take some time to work out and begin but the work is all in the setting up. After that, you gain so much time since you're not doing it all. Thirdly, you have to accept that some tasks will not be done to your exacting standards – and so what? Get your priorities right: does it matter that the dusting is done so the house gleams all day every day, or that you can sit down and share a coffee with your kids and chat because you don't have to do it all? But suggest that all of you think about the natural consequences. The natural consequence of you doing all the chores is that you are tired, resentful and not available to talk or play with them. The natural consequence of them doing a task badly is that you're upset and that they don't have a clean cup or a clean shirt for school. Once they begin to see that not doing what is required actually affects them, and you, then they will pull their weight. All it needs is for you keep faith in yourself and them, and hold the line. Good luck!

How should you draw up a chore chart?

For it to be something that everyone 'buys into' and agrees, it's best to make it a cooperative effort. But it does help for one person in the family to take responsibility for managing it and making it run. That doesn't have to be you, you can delegate this to a child as a way of further enlisting their cooperation and sense of ownership. To forestall arguments you could rotate this, asking each child to take responsibility for a week or a month at a time.

Have a family discussion and agree the following:

- What the routine chores are that you all think need doing. These could be washing up or feeding and walking pets, filling the dishwasher, loading the washing machine, laying tables, vacuuming the living room etc.

- Decide which chores have to be done, whatever happens. Different families have different ideas of what's important, so come to your own agreement.

- Decide which chores are quick and easy, which are long and hard.

- Draw up a list of chores, and assign them. You might like to give everyone a mixture of easy, medium and hard chores each week. Or you might opt for each person having easy, medium or hard weeks. You'll find some children like and even fight for some chores or hate others, and not everyone will hold the same views. You might opt for everyone having their set chores from then on or rotating so everyone gets a go at all of them, with some allowance for age, height and weight. Whatever scheme you decide, share out chores equally. That's the essence of being in a family: everyone pulls their weight and does their bit.

- You might also want to agree on what might be 'extra' chores, such as washing cars or mowing lawns, and negotiate whether these can be done as paid-for jobs. Some families may want to tie chores into pocket money – you get it if you complete your chores, or the amount you get is dependent on chores. You may want to consider whether this introduces an element of 'shall I, shan't I?' into the equation. Children wouldn't be very amused if Mum or Dad felt it depended on how they felt that day as to whether they got their evening meal or not. In the same light, whether or not you do your chores should be approached as similarly non-negotiable. Everyone does chores. End of story.

At what age can they do which chores?

You may have your own ideas about this and it's something you can discuss with your children and assess for yourself. As a generally agreed guide, children can:

At two to three:
put toys away
put dirty clothes in the laundry basket
help feed a pet
pick out their own clothes.

At four to five:
feed a pet
clean up spillages
get dressed
make their bed
clear the table after a meal
help empty the dishwasher.

At six to seven:
sort laundry
sweep a floor
set the table
help make meals
clean their bedroom.

At eight to nine:
load the dishwasher
put away groceries
put away laundry
walk the dog
prepare their breakfast (and yours too, on Mother's or Father's Day!).

At ten to twelve:
wash the car
do the laundry
iron clothes.

As teenagers:
make a meal
do the shopping
clean the bathroom and kitchen.

Agree what you're going to do, and then draw up a written agreement or contract setting it out. Ask everyone to sign the contract: 'We, the undersigned, agree...' Review the contract regularly and if it's not working, go back to the table to discuss why and what you'd like to do to make it work.

Getting a safe foundation

There are, of course, particular complexities to life as a lone parent. Being strong and coping with a life on your own is sometimes hard. If you don't have kids and only have yourself and the cat to look after when you break up with someone, you may allow yourself to collapse in a sodden puddle and wail that you can't possibly manage on your own. But even though you feel robbed of willpower and incapable of dealing with the big bad world on your own, when you have kids you are forced into a more adult mode. You may be all at sea with finances and confused with issues you've never had to cope with before but you are slightly more likely to get on and do it if you need to look after and protect your kids. Perhaps the first step of getting it together is to get your home on track. Once you have a foundation, and a safe bolthole that is yours and your family's, you can go out and tackle the world.

Summary

- Begin as you mean to go on. Give your home, and yourself, a makeover as an indication and a confirmation of your family's new start.
- Learn how to choose your battles when you talk, discuss or argue. Don't give the same weight or emotion to the trivial as to the all-important.
- The best way to spread the load is to use techniques like the chore chart so that everyone, adult and child, does their bit.
- Making your home a safe and secure foundation for all of you means you can move on and tackle anything together.

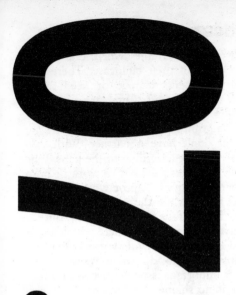

07

childcare

In this chapter you will learn:

- that every parent needs help with caring for their child at times
- how to work out what you need from childcare
- who can help you get what you want
- about leaving older children alone or in charge of a younger sibling
- about assessing what types of childcare could be best for you
- how to take up childcare – the questions to ask
- the finances of childcare.

Sorting out childcare

Every parent – even in two-parent families where one parent stays at home – needs to sort out their childcare. There will always be times when arrangements change or need to be flexible, or you both want some time off. Childcare is an even more vital issue when you're a lone parent. Making sure your children are looked after at all times and affording childcare are so much harder when you don't have a partner. With two parents you can cover each other, each filling in the gaps. One of you stays at home while the other goes out to work or both of you work and you either can afford help or work part-time or shifts so one of you is home while the other is out. Now you're on your own, it may feel as if it's all down to you. But for all the anxiety you may have about childcare there are plenty of ways of having your child looked after while you work, train, retrain or play – you just have to do some research and planning. Perhaps the most important issue to sort out for and with yourself is this: there is no shame in asking for help with your children, no brownie points to be gained by struggling on alone. Whatever you may believe, whatever you may think you can see around you, nobody manages alone.

Think about that old proverb 'It takes a village to raise a child.' It says it all. It means that children vastly benefit from input from many people, all around them – their parents, grandparents, other relatives, friends and neighbours. Add to that, in our more sophisticated society, various healthcare and education professionals. Children may gain immeasurably from your close, intimate relationship with them and from being with you. But they do best when they have a chance from an early age and all the way through their childhood to develop relationships with others and enjoy the variety and stimulation that comes from shared care. It also means that parents should and could profit from the help that is out there, not only informal, community and family help, but also that available from a wide network of official and voluntarily agencies. Many parents, and particularly single parents, feel guilty about the idea of leaving their children in another person's hands, as if not being there 24/7 yourself shows a dereliction of duty or incompetence. It shows neither.

There are plenty of arguments about the various merits of childcare and whether early years' care should be the sole preserve of close family or whether daily reliance on nursery or childminders has any harmful effect on small children. What seems to be the majority view is that the *quality* of the childcare is the key. Small children need *consistency*. You need to be sure they would be getting exactly the same attention, love and stimulation as they would get at home, and that outside childcare hours they are getting plenty of opportunity to be with you to build up your intimate bond with them. Children do benefit from an early age from the communal aspect of good childcare – meeting other adults and children, learning to be social and to get on, learning about new places, new people, new toys and games. Research suggests:

- Good quality childcare and early education give children a head start in primary school, because they support better educational, emotional and social development.
- Children who have good quality childcare outside their own home are likely to be more independent, better able to concentrate and more sociable at the start of primary school than children who stay at home.

So if you are delaying a return to work, or taking up work, now you are a single parent you may want to review that. Childcare can be flexible and tailored. So too, now, can training and working so that you can design your own training or working package around whatever childcare is available in your area.

What do you and your child need?

When you're organizing childcare, you need to work out what would suit you and your child best. You might find it helps to think about the following things:

- What sort of childcare do you and your child need at this point in their life – babysitting, something with a stimulating educational content for a pre-schooler, out-of-school hours minding or opportunities for activities, holiday care?
- When will you need it – days, evening or at nights and at set times or different times each week?
- How much can you afford – and don't forget holidays may cost more.
- Your child's needs and tastes – and don't forget these may change and will certainly evolve as they grow. What suits now will not next year.
- Where it is – near work or home or wherever you're learning or training.

Even if you have a set work or studying timetable you need some flexibility, not least because this timetable may change. Consider what will happen if you or the person looking after your child is ill. What if you need childcare in a hurry, for extra days or hours and at a different time from usual? What about holiday time? So when you're deciding what your main arrangement will be, make sure you have backup and a good support network as well.

Who could help with childcare?

Friends and family

One advantage of this arrangement is that they can be on call day or night, your place or theirs. They can be flexible, are known by you and your child and the arrangement is informal and so is less hassle. It's free or cheap – you may just be offering expenses – and friends and family are suitable helpers for any age of child. The disadvantage may be that you can't call the shots if you aren't paying and people may not be available when you need or want them. Your child carer may feel able to cancel when it suits them or withdraw help at short notice. Grandparents may be keen to help with a baby or small child and less able to cope with a boisterous pre-teen. Some relatives, godparents or friends may be less able to manage small children but delighted to offer a day out every half-term and holiday once the child is older.

The child's other parent

You may no longer be partners but they are still a parent to your children. The big advantage is that since it should be an equal responsibility, it's harder for a parent to excuse themselves from taking their share than a friend who has their own life to run. Children benefit enormously from having regular, frequent contact with both parents, so building contact visits into childcare arrangements can cover all bases. You and the other parent could share out pre- and after-school duties, holiday care and sick leave from work, as well as some evening and weekend care to give you a break to do your own thing. It's free, although how much time your child spends with the other parent would impact on the amount of maintenance paid to you – see Chapter 08 for more details. Again, the other parent can be there for you whatever the age of the child. The disadvantage is that arguments between you can spill over into this time and parents may let their children down in an effort to get back at the other adult. Both of you may have sudden and urgent calls on your time at the exact moment your child needs looking after, and you are the one likely to be left 'holding the baby'.

A registered childminder

They look after your child along with other children in their own home. Some offer flexible hours, so can care for children all or part of the day. The advantage is planned care when you want it and with someone who is registered and checked, although not necessarily trained. All childminders in the UK must be registered and inspected by the Office for Standards in Education (Ofsted). They will carry out regular checks on the childminder and their home and make sure that all adults living and working in the childminder's home are also police and health checked. Childminders are best for pre-school children but will also look after primary school age children before or after school and during school holidays. The disadvantage can be costs and flexibility – some may only want to offer help during the working weekday and not during school holidays.

A nanny

Nannies provide childcare in your own home. The big advantage of a nanny is that she (or sometimes he) will fit in with unusual working hours, might live in and could work part-time. Some families find it particularly useful to share a nanny between them so you have a regular part-time worker but she has a full-time job. Some may agree to do cooking and tidying as well as looking after children. The disadvantage is that they can be expensive. In the UK, nannies can have a recognized childcare qualification or nursery nurse training, but they don't have to have one to offer themselves as a nanny – the salary you negotiate may reflect this. Nannies, unlike registered childminders, are not inspected by Ofsted. But they can apply to the Childcare Approval Scheme through Sure Start and will have to meet basic criteria before being approved, and you may want to find one who is approved (see Taking it further for more details). As well as wages, you would have to pay their tax and national insurance contributions, holiday and sick pay. Nannies usually look after pre-school or primary school children.

Au pairs

Au pairs are young women or men from all over Europe who come to the UK to study English. In exchange for bed and board and the experience of living with a family in this country they can help out in the home with child care and light cleaning duties, for a maximum of five hours a day. As well as working for some of their keep, au pairs must be given two days off a week, a weekly allowance of around £50, meals and their own room. Since they are not registered or usually trained to work with children they are really only suitable for minding school age children but can be a good option when it comes to providing affordable pre- and after-school care, and some evening, weekend and holiday cover. The advantages of having an au pair is that they are an inexpensive live-in option with flexible hours. Au pairs may remain an option even when children are into secondary school and you simply want someone to be there when they get back from school or during evenings, some weekends and holidays. They can provide your child with valuable learning experiences, living with and getting to know someone from a different culture, a different country and speaking a different language.

Pre-school playgroups

A pre-school or playgroup offers play and education sessions lasting about three to four hours for children between three and five years old, often accompanied by a parent, either every day or on several days a week during term time. Groups are organized by the community or voluntary groups on a not-for-profit basis, often with help from parents. A registered pre-school or playgroup would be regularly inspected by Ofsted. Some pre-school playgroups are developing their services to offer longer sessions or full-time day-care. The advantages are that your use of them can be very flexible, making them part of your extended childcare. They can be inexpensive and a good way to join in with other parents in your community.

Nursery schools and classes

Nursery schools and nursery classes provide early education and childcare for children between three and five years old. Some schools and classes are part of the state education system, others are run by private or voluntary sector organizations and they offer structured play and learning activities suitable for the age of the child. The advantages are that you would be leaving your child in a regularly inspected environment with qualified teachers and nursery assistants. The disadvantages may be cost (the fees vary across the country) and inflexibility. Nursery schools are generally open during school hours, normally only in term time, usually from 9 a.m. to 3.30 p.m. for full- or half-day sessions. Some may also offer out-of-school care before or after school during term time and in the school holidays.

Day nurseries

A day nursery provides care and education for children between the ages of six weeks and five years, and many also offer out-of-school care for five- to eleven-year-olds. Day nurseries can be run by the council, the community, based in the work place or privately run. As with nursery schools, the advantages of a day nursery are that your child will be able to experience learning and development activities suitable for their age with qualified teachers and assistants. The disadvantage may be cost and inflexibility. Day nurseries are generally open longer hours than nursery schools, usually coinciding with a standard working day – 8 a.m. to 7 p.m. on weekdays, 50 weeks of the year, but offering no cover on evenings or weekends. You can send your child full- or part-time.

Sure Start children's centres

Sure Start children's centres are being developed across the UK. They will provide a range of services to parents and children, including childcare along with early education and health services for children under five years old. They may also offer family support, a base for childminders, and links with Jobcentre Plus, Children's Information Services (CIS) and also further education institutions. They are open a minimum of 48 weeks a year, five days a week, ten hours a day. By 2010 there will be one for every community – 2,500 of them are open already. Many centres will be developed from Sure Start local programmes, Neighbourhood Nurseries and Early Excellence Centres and involve private/voluntary provision. Advantages will be flexibility and the range of services you can access from one centre, and that all centres will be checked and inspected by Ofsted.

A work or college crèche

Some workplaces and colleges offer their own crèche to care for pre-school children while their parents are on the premises, during the working or college day. The advantage is support and fun for your child where you are, so there is no extra travel involved and you're on hand if your child needs you. The disadvantage is that the care is only available while you are at work (although that might be an advantage, too, since it makes sure you don't get pressured into working late!) and sometimes cost, and waiting lists.

School-based childcare

Many schools are now offering a range of services to support parents and pupils well beyond the usual school hours or term times. Most have always offered activities such as music, art or sport clubs or additional study support after normal school hours, which can function as after-school childcare. Often these are based on school sites but they may also be in youth clubs, community centres and nurseries. More and more schools now offer breakfast clubs (normally open from 8 a.m.) in addition to the after-school clubs (which typically run from 3.30 p.m. to 6 p.m.) and holiday play schemes (8 a.m. to 6 p.m.) out of term time. As a result schools may be open from 8 a.m. to 6 p.m., even during the holidays. These are not additional learning classes held by teachers, but either childcare organized by the school or provided by local voluntary groups, private providers and childminders, who provide staff and sometimes facilities. It's projected that by 2010 all schools will provide such extra activities, available from at least 8 a.m. to 6 p.m. before and after the school day and in most of the holidays, offering cover for 48 weeks a year. The advantages of such services are that they are on-site, you don't have to arrange travel between childminder and school, and they are in the company of your child's friends.

Looking after themselves

Once children get to a certain age, you can rely on them to get themselves to and from school, to look after themselves responsibly between their coming home and you arriving, and on some evenings and for some periods over weekends. Indeed, some children may welcome a chance to have the home to themselves for a short time. You may need to negotiate with them what happens when they look after themselves – what they do, who they see, where they might go. It can be difficult thrashing this out with a pre-teen or teenager who is testing their ability to look after themselves, sometimes with more enthusiasm than sense, but it may be an important part of helping them grow up. Older children can often be relied on to mind younger siblings, for a time. Apart from the obvious advantage of this being free, it also gives your children the chance to take responsibility for themselves and to manage relationships with younger siblings, to make themselves a snack or begin to prepare the evening meal for you, and to do homework without your nagging. The disadvantage is that you have to balance convenience with safety and judge when children are old enough. You'll want to discuss:

- **Safety** – are you confident they know how to be alone in the home without burning it down or flooding it?
- **Protection** – are you happy they know how to deal with people coming to the door or calling on the phone?
- **Nutrition** – are you satisfied they know what they should and should not be stuffing themselves with until you get back?
- **Responsibility at home** – are you agreed on what chores they may be expected to do at this time?
- **Responsibility elsewhere** – have you established a homework protocol so they know when it should be done even if you're not there?

When are children old enough to be left at home alone?

The law does not say when it is legal to leave a child on their own, but if anything happens and it is decided you left the child 'in a manner likely to cause unnecessary suffering or injury to health' you could be prosecuted for wilful neglect. Whether you leave a child on their own, for a few minutes or several hours, you need to consider:

- their age
- how mature they may be
- where you are leaving them and if the area is secure and safe
- how long you're going to be gone
- how often you plan to do this
- whether the child is alone or with someone else.

Babies and toddlers should never be left alone in a house when you are not there, even for a few minutes, even if they are sound asleep and even if you think the place is secure. They may wake up, they may become distressed and a toddler may head straight into danger. As a rough guide you shouldn't really leave a child under the age of 13 alone, except for a very short time and under certain conditions, set out below.

- Talk it through carefully with your child and make sure they are happy and confident for you to go.
- Discuss safety at home and make sure dangerous materials are out of reach or locked up.
- Set agreed rules about internet access and programmes they can watch while you are gone.
- Always leave a phone number and be on the end of it.
- Agree with your child that they will keep the home door locked and will not answer to strangers.
- Make sure they know what to do in an emergency and how to ring the emergency services. Tell them never to make a hoax call but be clear that the emergency services would rather they were called when not really needed than not be called when they were.
- Leave a list of people you trust who they can call if necessary.
- Tell the child what time you'll return, and be on time or call.
- Talk it through afterwards – how did it go, how did they feel?

With teenagers, it is likely to be appropriate to leave them regularly between getting home from school and you coming home, and for the occasional evening. Be guided by your own instincts and the child – talking it through with them will reveal any problems and allow you to make a judgement of their level of maturity and what they may be ready to manage. You do need to go through all the above issues with them, and revisit them from time to time to make sure the young person is happy.

What childcare should you choose?

Each type of childcare has its pros and cons, and you'll need to work out what is best for you and your family. The hours you need it, what you can afford but most importantly what suits your children will be part of your calculation. Most likely, you will find a combination works best, with several back-ups since virtually every provision will fail sooner or later, if only once!

From the postbag

I have an extra job in the evenings to pay for the little extras we all need. My 15-year-old seems fine about it although sometimes he seems moody when I'm getting ready to go. My ten-year-old hates it – he plays up and says his brother bosses him around. I've tried to explain we couldn't go on holiday if I didn't do the extra but he says he doesn't care. How can I get him to understand?

Actually, I'm with your son. Children prize, and need, your attention and time with you far more than holidays away. Leaving even a teenager alone regularly can leave them feeling abandoned and rejected. Of course the older brother is bossy – he's been put in the position of parent and feels it's his job to look after his younger sibling since you're not there to do it. And of course he is moody – he misses you too and probably resents having to be so responsible at such a young age. Both can manage perfectly well after school and before you come home from your main job. But leaving them most evenings is not helping them at this age. Forgo the little extras for the next few years and spend time with them. It will pay off. Good luck!

Essential points

- Your childcare needs are likely to be varied and changing.
- There is a wide range of childcare options available, ranging from friends and family, childminders, nannies, au pairs, playgroups, nurseries, children's centres, work crèches and schools to trusting children to look after themselves.
- The best option may be to organize a variety of care, tailor-made to fit you and your family.

There is a wealth of childcare out there – and loads of ways to find it. Your local Children's Information Service (CIS) can tell you what's available – you'll find one in your area. See the Taking it further section at the end of this book for the contact details for CIS and other organizations that could help. Most childcare options get booked up quickly. College and work crèches, nurseries and good childminders are often in great demand. As soon as you know your plans, get your child's name down for the ones you want.

Taking up childcare

Leaving your child with someone else can be difficult and stressful at first. Set your mind at rest by getting the arrangements straight.

- Consider your and your child's needs – what you'll need, where and when; and what will suit them now and in the future.
- Plan ahead. Give yourself plenty of time to make your choice and start looking as soon as you realize you'll need it. It can take months to find and interview nannies and other home carers and popular options can have waiting lists.
- Always have a back-up plan especially if you're relying on family. Things may change for them and however much they want to help they may suddenly be unable to do so.
- Research all the options – contact your local Children's Information Service (CIS) for a list of registered childcare in your community.
- Shop around. Everyone looking after children will understand the necessity to get it right and not be insulted at being visited to be checked out. They will recognize that it can be a matter of taste – what is right for one child may not suit another. Visit at least two or three places to meet the carer and compare what's on offer. Make a formal appointment during care time so you can see how the children already there behave, and take a list of prepared questions. Where possible, drop in unannounced at a time of your choice to see exactly what happens when they are not expecting you.
- Consider a range of care. If none of what you find offers exactly the cover you need, merge what is on offer and tailor it to fit you.
- Check references, registration, public liability and first aid certificates and get in touch with other mothers to see what they have experienced. Carers should be happy to give you names of other parents to speak to about their work.
- Check and check again. Go back for a second or third look once you've narrowed down your choices. This gives you the time to confirm that they meet all your requirements. Some carers will agree to trial runs before a formal agreement, to see how it's going to work out.
- Get it all in writing once a decision has been made. Nurseries will ask you to sign a contract or letter, outlining details such

as costs, rules, hours, etc. Read it carefully before signing. Put together your own for anyone who does not have one, such as a nanny or some childminders. See Taking it further for links to find a suggested contract.

Questions to ask

These may be some of the questions to ask the person or the organization that will be looking after your child:

- What qualifications do carers have?
- Are there any other adults there – who are they and how often will they be there?
- What times can you take my child – and can you be flexible?
- Would it cost extra and would you need to be told in advance if I needed a longer day?
- What happens if I'm late to collect?
- What happens if you can't take my child on a particular day because of illness or for other reasons?
- How much notice do you need for holidays?
- What toys do you have, what games and other activities do you offer?
- What will children be doing when they're with you?
- How many other children will be there too – are they regular?
- Do you take the children out and do you tell me in advance when this happens?
- How will you manage my child's particular needs – what they eat, when they rest, how they behave?
- Do we agree on what sort of food is available to them, what TV or other media they can view, what they should be learning and how you discipline them or encourage good behaviour?
- How much will it cost – are there extra costs for any items or activities?
- What payment arrangements do we make if you're ill or when we go on holiday?
- When and how should I pay?

Paying for childcare

Paying for childcare can take a big chunk out of your household income. However, don't rule out any options until you've worked out what financial help is available.

Free childcare

All three- and four-year-olds are entitled to free part-time early education. This means two-and-a-half hours of early education a day, five days a week, 33 weeks a year, available from the first term following your child's third birthday. Free part-time places can be in school nursery classes or reception classes in a state or private nursery school, or in a day nursery, a playgroup or pre-school group or with a childminder who is part of an approved Childminder Network. For information on what's available in your area and how to claim your child's free early education, contact your local Children's Information Service (CIS) via ChildcareLink (see Taking it further).

Getting help with childcare costs if you're at work

About one in ten employers provide some kind of childcare help to employees, such as supplying childcare allowances and vouchers, and running subsidized workplace crèches and nurseries. Childcare vouchers can be used to pay for care provided by registered or approved childminders, nurseries and after-school groups. You exchange part of your salary in return for the vouchers, and save the National Insurance deducted from £50 per week, and the tax from £50 per week as well so it actually works out that you're taking home more money. Contact your local Children's Information Service (CIS) for more information.

Working parents are also eligible for tax credits, and the Childcare Tax Credit pays towards registered childcare.

Tax credits

Tax credits are regular payments to help you with your bills. You don't need to pay taxes to be able to claim Tax Credits. You get Tax Credits weekly or monthly, paid straight into your bank, building society, Post Office or National Savings Account. It's not taken off a tax bill if you pay tax. Nine out of ten families are eligible for financial help, depending on their circumstances.

If you have a child living with you who is under 16, or under 19 and in full-time education and your family income is less than £58,175 a year (£66,350 if a child is under 1) you may qualify for Child Tax Credit, which is paid on top of Child Benefit. It's worth over £32 a week for one child, and goes up with more children. If you have a child with a disability you can receive extra help.

If you have a child of school-age or under living with you and work 16 hours a week or more and are on low pay, you may qualify for Working Tax Credit. You can claim if you work for someone else or are self-employed. Working Tax Credit is paid through your pay packet on top of Child Benefit and Child Tax Credit. The Childcare Element of Working Tax Credit is specifically aimed at helping working parents cover childcare costs. You can claim up to a maximum of 80 pence for every £1 you pay for registered or approved childcare up to certain limits. From April 2005, the limit is £175 a week for one child, and £300 for two or more.

As long as your nanny or childminder is registered or approved through the Childcare Approval Scheme you are entitled to financial support to help pay for child care through Working Tax Credit and Employer Supported Childcare tax and NICs exemptions.

If you're studying or retraining

Lone parents can get allowances for childcare to help them return to learning, train for a new job or look for work. New Deal for Lone Parents will offer you a personal adviser who can inform and help you – see Taking it further for contact details.

There are access and hardship funds available through some colleges. Failing that, there are grants from charitable trusts or student loans. Your personal adviser can direct and help you – see Taking it further for contact details.

College crèches or nurseries are often low cost but they do get booked up quickly so if you are thinking of going for more qualifications it would be advisable to check out the on-site childcare as soon as possible.

In the USA

For more information on choosing safe and healthy child care if you are in the USA, find/contact your local child care resource and referral agency by consulting Child Care Aware, a national consumer education parent hotline. Their website is at **www.childcareaware.org** or you can call them toll free on 1-800-424-2246. Or contact the National Child Care Information Centre (NCCIC), which is a national clearing-house and technical assistance centre that links parents, providers, policy-makers, researchers, and the public to early care and education information. Their website is **www.nccic.org** or you can call them on 1-800-616-2242.

Essential points

- Childcare needs to be researched and planned ahead with plenty of time to spare.
- You should feel able to ask questions and check out any child care provider and their premises.
- Financial help is available to pay for childcare – explore what is available before ruling out any option.

Case study

How much can you get to help you with childcare from tax credits? Ruth is a lone parent with two children, Jake aged 13 and Miriam aged two. She works 30 hours a week. In 2006/7 she earned £8,000 before tax and got £3,000 maintenance. She will still be in the same job in 2007/8 but expects to earn £8,500, and get the same maintenance. Ruth pays a childminder £80 a week to look after Miriam.

Ruth will get, annually:

The **Family Element** of Child Tax Credit = £545

For each child a **Child Element** of Child Tax Credit – £1,765 x 2 = £3530

The **Basic Element** of Working Tax Credit = £1665

The **Lone Parent Element** of Working Tax Credit = £1640

The **30-hour Element** of Working Tax Credit = £680

The **Childcare Element** of Working Tax Credit – 80 per cent of 52 weeks x £80 = £3328. (The Childcare Element is worked out as an average cost over 52 weeks, even if you only pay for childcare for some weeks in the year.)

Ruth's Tax Credit comes to a **total** of £11,388.

Does Ruth get this full amount? Maintenance doesn't count but the fact she gets more than £5220 a year for her 16 hours work a week does. The £5,220 is what is called a threshold figure – earn more and some of the extra is taken off your award.

Summary

- Children can benefit from carefully chosen childcare from an early age even if the parent is at home full-time.
- When planning your childcare, explore the full range of possibilities – family, friends, the other parent and commercial or community-based schemes.
- Before considering leaving a child on their own or in charge of younger siblings, talk it through with them to assess their maturity and how they feel about it.
- Each type of childcare has its pros and cons and having a variety is often useful. If you do have a choice, consider and plan thoroughly before coming to a decision, and recognize that your and your child's needs will change over the years.

08

money matters

In this chapter you will learn:
- about financial responsibility towards your children's upkeep
- the significance of money – it does more than simply pay the bills
- how to manage finances between you and the other parent
- how to calculate maintenance and who can help you with this
- about taking paid employment or not – the benefits you can claim and how to do so
- the best ways of managing debt or borrowing
- how to manage budgets and how to involve your child.

Sorting out finances

Finances can be a tricky issue in any family – doubly so when one parent is managing on their own. Child maintenance and support, budgets and allowances can all be a nightmare to negotiate alone, particularly if you managed without too many problems before you became a lone parent. Single parents come from every background, every age, every earning level and all jobs and professions and you may be lucky enough to be in a job that earns you enough to pay the bills or to have sufficient money behind you. On the other hand, you may be one of the very many lone parents who struggle to make ends meet.

Being a lone parent is demonstrably bad for your wallet. Single parents are three times more likely to live in rented accommodation than traditional families. You are also more likely to fall into debt. You may have to rely on maintenance which may be unreliable (less than one-third of single parents receive child maintenance), have a low income or have had to give up a job to care for your children and thus had to rely on benefits. One extra expense can spell disaster. The good news is that it doesn't have to be like that. There is support available, and this is where you can find out about making the changes that will help you. So how can you manage?

The other parent's financial responsibilities

Even though you may be bringing up children on your own you should not be paying for them on your own. If the other parent is alive, they should be paying child maintenance. Child maintenance is the money that both parents contribute towards their child's day-to-day expenses. The non-resident parent should expect to give a sum towards the everyday living costs of a child living with the parent with residence. Contact and maintenance are, and should be, entirely separate. Paying up does not give extra rights for contact, nor does refusing contact mean the parent need not pay.

Children are always the responsibility of both their parents whether those parents live together or apart. Parents are parents for the rest of their lives and children look to them for love, support and care whether contact is daily, occasional or not at all. As far as the legal system is concerned, a parent remains financially liable for their children until they are 18, whatever the contact arrangements. Most parents, of course, continue contributing to and subsidizing their children well beyond this.

Money can be a source of bitterness in single parent families because it can provide a continuing reminder of how abandoned and rejected the family may feel, struggling to manage on very little while the other parent appears not to care. Being able to afford to pay bills may not be the only issue.

The significance of money

Money is like food or presents: it's one of those things that often stands in for something else. Lovers and parents set forth tasty treats and luxurious meals as a way of showing love, attention and commitment. Presents are given as a way of assuring the recipient that you care and they matter. In families that have undergone change, money may be given as a way of assuring or reassuring children that the missing parent is still on the scene. More often, money may be requested or demanded and pursued for much more than its simple ability to pay bills. It can be seen as a form of revenge. The missing parent may be seen to have cheated in taking themselves away, but at least the abandoned parent may demand a form of presence, or dish out punishment, by taking their cash. Or the motive may be sadness rather than anger and the money may be seen as a reassurance that the missing person is still committed to the family.

For the parent paying maintenance, money can be seen as a way of exerting control from a distance. Some non-residential parents may be very generous with the amount they offer but with strings attached. The relationship may outwardly be over, but it actually continues through the conditions imposed along with the cheques.

Money and contact may often be seen as conditional, one upon the other. The inference being that if you don't pay you can't see. In retaliation this may be interpreted as 'If I can't see when and how I like, I won't pay.'

Managing finances between you and the other parent

If you want to manage finances when you are a single parent, you should:

- Separate emotional issues from financial ones. Are disagreements and demands over money actually about leftover anger or pain? Before you talk about money it might be useful for ex-partners to use counselling to seek closure. Have your final say, be reassured the other has listened and heard you, and then move on.

- Separate money from any other issue. Money is necessary to pay bills and to reassure children that their parents still see them as their responsibility. If one parent needs to let the other know they are hurt, angry or disappointed, say it, don't use covert means such as manipulating financial or contact arrangements to pass on the message.

- Separate adult needs from children's. Adults need money to care for children, but as far as children are concerned the only priority is staying in contact. Don't jeopardize or affect one with arguments or actions over the other.

Maintenance

How do you decide the amount of maintenance that should be paid to you? There are two ways for maintenance to be set up between separated parents. The first, and in many ways the best, is as a private arrangement between you. This can be as an informal arrangement or as a formal written agreement. A parenting plan can give you a framework for working this out between you (see Taking it further). The issues that you might like to consider in discussing finances between you would be:

- What amounts should be paid towards day-to-day living expenses by the non-resident parent?
- How will travel for contact visits be paid for?
- How will special expenses such as school trips or large purchases such as computers, bicycles or mobile phones be paid for?
- How much pocket money will children receive and from whom?
- How will you renegotiate and adjust financial matters if circumstances change?

To assess expenses you would need to take into account the non-resident parent's income, how many nights the child regularly stays with them, how many children the non-resident parent is paying maintenance for, and how many they have living with them. When calculating the amount of child maintenance owed by a non-resident parent, any children who live with them – their own from a new relationship and stepchildren – are taken into account.

Pros and cons of voluntary agreements

There are advantages and disadvantages to making a voluntary agreement between you. Advantages are:

- Personal negotiation avoids conflict. Involving other people or statutory agencies can feel confrontational and keep parties at arm's length, where misunderstandings can occur and blow up into arguments.
- Arrangements can easily and quickly be altered to meet a changing situation.
- What is thought mutually fair and agreed is what is paid.

Disadvantages are:

- You and the other parent need to communicate to arrive at a mutually acceptable result. If there is hostility or any lingering feelings of abandonment or pain it may be hard to meet face to face or to keep discussions objective.
- If an informal agreement breaks down, you may have difficulty in enforcing it.

If a voluntary agreement breaks down, a court is likely to confirm it if it was recorded and properly witnessed. For this reason it is always a good idea to have a solicitor's help in drawing up an agreement and to have it signed and witnessed. A family solicitor who is a member of Resolution (see Taking it further) and who will encourage agreement rather than confrontation would be the best choice to guide parents through the process.

Applying for maintenance

In the UK, the other way to apply for child maintenance is to go through the government agency that calculates and collects child maintenance and enforces its payment. This was the Child Support Agency, replaced in 2008 by the Child Maintenance and Enforcement Commission (CMEC). The Commission can offer help to parents agreeing child maintenance in various ways. It can help parents calculate what maintenance should be, depending on the number of children concerned, the income of the non-resident parent, the amount of time children spend with that parent and the number of children who live with that parent. This can be done via an on-line tool, on the phone or face to face. Asking the Commission for help in calculating maintenance does not mean you have to ask them to collect it for you. The idea is to help parents make their own choices about how to manage finances between you. The preference is always for you to make your own private arrangements because the reality is that when this happens, discussion and continued payment usually goes more smoothly. However, you have the option at any time to ask the CMEC to step in to enforce the payment of the maintenance which they have calculated.

Advantages of using the CMEC are:

- Parents don't have to communicate if this has become difficult.
- The CMEC will do all the hard work, calculating the amount to be paid and collecting it.
- If money is not paid, the CMEC will pursue it.

Disadvantages of using the CMEC are:

- Any conflict between parents is not resolved and may increase.
- Settlements imposed by outside authority tend to be resisted and resented.
- Neither parent has any control over the amount awarded.
- The amount given may be slow to be changed if the situation alters.

In the USA, arrangements for child support are run by the individual states and may vary. The Administration for Children and Families, the division of the Department for Health and Human Services that is responsible for Child Support, suggests that to find the forms you need for child support services, you should check your state child support website. State websites are available at **www.acf.hhs.gov/programs/cse/extinf.htmf** (or **http://tinyurl.com/39jwfj**). Or you can call your state Child Support Enforcement Agency and ask how to get the forms you need. Agency addresses and telephone numbers are at: **http://ocse.acf.hhs.gov/int/directories/index.cfm?fuseaction=m ain.extivdlist** (or **http://tinyurl.com/2t4xzc**).

Case study

When Kim and Justin broke up, he made generous but irregular payments towards the upkeep of their daughter, Eleanor. He also saw her every weekend and at least one night a week. After a year he started seeing someone and when they moved in together, Justin cancelled a few weekends and was occasionally late on making payments. Eleanor was hurt but Kim was furious and after one particularly bitter row over money, she told him that if he didn't pay at once, and enough to cover the money she felt he'd short-changed them on in the past, he could forget about seeing Eleanor again. Justin was incensed and having written a card to his daughter saying it wasn't his choice, stopped contact. After a few weeks, Kim was contacted by Eleanor's school. Her work and behaviour had significantly deteriorated. The teacher who Kim saw was a single parent herself and very sympathetic. She was also very supportive of the idea that Kim should seek mediation with Justin and get the money situation settled, if for no other reason than Eleanor's happiness. Kim contacted National Family Mediation and invited Justin to attend. To her surprise, he came eagerly – he had missed his daughter, felt bad about the situation and wanted it sorted. They agreed to the mediator's suggestion, to have the CMEC set a fair amount of maintenance and for it to be in the shape of a monthly standing order. The amount settled on was less in some respects than the irregular amounts Justin had been giving, but overall about the same, and paid regularly and consistently. More importantly, both apologized to Eleanor and owned up to having behaved badly and she and her father resumed their regular contact.

Emotional effects of financial difficulties in single parent families

When dealing with financial matters it is absolutely essential to first sort out any emotional ramifications. If there are either arguments over money or resentment or hurt feelings around it you need to sit down and sort out:

- what you are really feeling
- what are the real issues behind your emotions
- what you might like to be different
- what you might have to settle for.

Once the underlying emotions behind an objection are brought out and discussed you may be able to make arrangements that are both fair and acceptable. Simply being able to voice a degree of understandable resentment, jealousy or confusion can actually make those feelings far more manageable.

Essential points

- Both parents have a legal as well as moral duty to maintain their children even if they no longer live with them.
- Money is more than a means to pay bills. It also has emotional significance.
- We can use money to convey value, and exert control.
- Maintenance can be agreed voluntarily between separated parents or collected by the government agency the CMEC. The CMEC can help by calculating the amount of maintenance owing even if you do not choose to have them involved for collection purposes.

Where else to go for financial help

You're entitled to help if money is scarce and you're on your own with a child. Receiving benefits doesn't mean you must be isolated. You can receive benefits and still share your home with your parents or other family members, friends or a gay partner. You can also claim as a lone parent if you share a home with an ex-partner, as long as you no longer live as a couple.

There are lots of different benefits and allowances. Getting one can depend on what's happening to you at that time and what other benefits you may be getting, so you need to remember to always check if a change occurs in your life because it may be that you could claim a new benefit, or have to give one up. The Department for Work and Pensions or DWP is the UK government department that deals with benefits. Jobcentre Plus is the agency where you make your benefit claims. Look in your local phone book for your local centre, or call via the helpline (see Taking it further) and ask them for help.

What can you claim if you're not working?

You can claim Income Support if you're not working, or work less than 16 hours a week. Ask your local Jobcentre Plus for an

Income Support Claim Pack. You should start being paid the week after you make your claim. If you need money at once, ask to have your claim treated as urgent or ask for a Crisis Loan to tide you over.

You also get health benefits and help with health costs. If you're on Income Support and you are pregnant or have a child under four, you are entitled to Healthy Start vouchers that can be exchanged for cow's milk (including infant formula milk) and fresh fruit and vegetables. You can also get free prescriptions, dental treatment, sight tests and glasses and fares to hospital. Your child gets free school meals and you may qualify for a grant for school uniform from the local education authority.

Will you be asked to find a job?

You may be asked to take part in an interview about work or training prospects as a condition of getting benefit. You have to go to the interview but if your youngest child is under 12 you will not have to accept work or training if you choose not to. The age has recently dropped from 16 and is likely to drop still further to seven by 2010.

Are there any other benefits you can claim?

If you're on Income Support, you can also claim Housing Benefit. If you're a council tenant, this goes straight into your housing account to pay your rent. If you rent privately, it's paid direct to you. You can also claim Council Tax Benefit, which reduces the amount of Council Tax you will be asked to pay. You fill in the forms in the claim pack you get from Jobcentre Plus and they forward them to the benefits section at your local council.

All parents get Child Benefit paid by Jobcentre Plus. You get this as a sum of money which is expected to go towards items you need for your child. You can also get some one-off grants or loans when a baby arrives or while you're bringing up your child. These are available from The Social Fund, which is part of Jobcentre Plus. If you're in need or have problems, you can ask for a grant:

- A Sure Start Maternity Grant is available to parents on Income Support, just before or when a baby arrives. It helps with the early costs of having a baby – buggy, cot, clothes, and so on.

- A Community Care Grant is for people coming out of care, or for anyone on Income Support under great pressure. For instance, if your place is cramped or in bad condition you can ask for help. You can also ask for help if someone in the family is ill or distressed or if there is violence and you have to move or replace items that have been broken or taken.

- A Budgeting Loan is a sum of money for items you might need and can't afford without help. You have to repay the loan out of your benefit but you don't pay interest. You should have been on Income Support for at least 26 weeks before you can ask for this.

Seven tips for making a claim

1 Write down the questions you want to ask so you don't forget them.

2 If you're making the claim in person, go as early as possible – you may have to wait and it can take some time.

3 If you can't get to the office, ask for someone to visit you.

4 Take a friend or family member to boost your morale and keep you company.

5 Keep a record of what was said and keep letters that they send to you.

6 Make sure you give the forms to the right person, and ask for a copy to show when and where you gave them in.

7 Don't forget to take ID, especially if you need cash on the spot.

What benefits are you entitled to if you're working?

In the UK, if you are working for 16 hours a week or more you can claim Working Families Tax Credit and Childcare Tax Credit for help with childcare costs. You can also claim Children's Tax Credit which is a tax allowance for any child under 16. All tax credits come from the Inland Revenue. They work out what you're due and the tax you'd otherwise have deducted decreases and you keep more in your pay packet.

Depending on what you earn, you may be entitled to Housing Benefit and Council Tax Benefit if you get Working Families Tax Credit. You apply through Jobcentre Plus and they send it on to your local council.

A Sure Start Maternity Grant is available to parents on Working Families Tax Credit, just before or when a baby arrives. It helps with the early costs of having a baby such as buggy, cot and clothes. If you receive Working Families Tax Credit, you also get free medicines, dental treatment, eye tests and vouchers for glasses.

Getting a job

The real problem with all these benefits, allowances and tax credits is knowing how to fit them together. Your earnings in a full-time job may give you more cash in hand than Income Support, for instance. But if you come off Income Support you may no longer be eligible for other benefits. This could leave you much worse off overall. One of the services Jobcentre Plus, Citizen's Advice Bureau and One Parent Families (see Taking it further) offer you is an adviser who can do a 'better off' calculation. Together you can work out what you'd gain and what you'd lose by getting training or a job. You can see if it's worthwhile financially. However, it's well worth considering the emotional benefits of training or taking up a job, which can outweigh the financial penalties. Having a job may help you to feel more in control of your life. It will make use of the many skills you have and allows you to develop more. That contributes to your self-confidence and self-esteem and helps you cope better with life both inside and outside the family. And it passes on a message to your children – that their parent is in control and has self-worth, which helps them too.

Finding help to get a job or training

You can apply to Jobcentre Plus for their New Deal for Lone Parents (NDLP). This is a special programme to help lone parents who are not working to get training or work. It offers some extra benefits to make it easier. You can join if you're a single parent and have been on Income Support and on other benefits for six months, and even if you already work as long as it's for less than 16 hours a week. If you apply, you'll be invited to a meeting with a NDLP adviser at a Jobcentre Plus – find your nearest centre in the phonebook or on the internet. If you have difficulties getting to a Jobcentre Plus, the adviser can come and see you.

The adviser will discuss training and job opportunities and will do a 'better off' calculation, and explain what benefits or tax credits you may be entitled to when you move into work. NDLP can help with childcare and travelling costs while you're training and looking for work and if you're on Income Support and take up training through NDLP you'll get an extra £15 a week 'Training Premium'. In addition, the CMEC will, if needed, fast track maintenance applications from you if you're actively seeking work.

Does all this help stop once I start work or training?

If you take a job, you can get a grant to cover paying in advance for childcare or other necessary costs to get you started. If it's a part-time job of less than 16 hours a week and you still need Income Support, you can go on getting help with childcare costs. The NDLP adviser can also arrange for the Inland Revenue to fast track Working Families Tax Credit once you've found work. Your adviser can continue giving some support even when you've found work.

Are there any special payments to make it worthwhile starting full-time work?

If you go into full-time work, you don't necessarily lose all your benefits at once. You may be able to claim an extra two weeks Income Support (called Lone Parents Run-On). You get this if you've been getting Income Support as a lone parent for at least 26 weeks and the job will last at least five weeks. Tell Jobcentre Plus when you will be starting work and they will tell you the last date you can use your order book or will get a payment into your bank account. You can also get an extra four weeks' Housing Benefit and Council Tax Benefit. These will be paid automatically if you get the Lone Parents Run-On. If you aren't on Income Support but do get Housing Benefit or Council Tax Benefit, you can still claim for the extended payment. You need to make a claim within four weeks of starting work or you may lose some benefit.

Back-to-work bonus

If you've been claiming Income Support for at least 91 days and had benefit reduced because of your part-time earnings, you might be able to get some of it back as a bonus for starting work.

Child maintenance bonus

If you were receiving child maintenance while on Income Support, you may qualify for a bonus when you come off benefit to start work. You must apply within 28 days of coming off benefits from your local Jobcentre Plus.

What if you decide you can't work yet?

If your youngest child is under 12 you can withdraw at any time. You don't have to accept a job if one is found for you or start work at the end of any training that you have through NDLP. Of course, if you get training and a job, the chances are your income will increase. You might get a promotion and other opportunities. Many employers give you more money or perks the longer you stay. Benefits, on the other hand, don't change much. So even if you might be worse off at first, it might be worth it. Talk and think it over.

What if you can't decide what job or course to take?

The personal adviser at Jobcentre Plus may be the best person to help you work this out. Remember, the job market has changed a lot in the last few years, and goes on changing. People move about from job to job and new skills are wanted. Perhaps you have been out of the employment scene for some time, being a parent and becoming a lone parent. It may have left you feeling lacking in skills and with your self-confidence dented. But your experiences will have also given you skills you didn't have before, skills that you may not realize you have. When you consider what sort of work you may be suited for it helps to sit down and have a realistic look at what you want and what you can do. You may want a job that:

- interests you
- challenges you
- gives you a social life
- gets you out the house
- shows your kids their parent is a Someone
- pays good money.

You may not think you have much to give, until you sit down and work it out. You're a parent, which means you can probably say that you can:

- listen
- organize
- budget
- take responsibility
- negotiate
- compromise.

Talking to a Jobcentre Plus adviser will help you to decide what you may want to do and how to go for it. You may need some help with:

- filling in application forms
- setting out your CV
- succeeding at interviews.

A Jobcentre Plus adviser can help with all of these and steer you in the right direction for learning courses, training or a job that's right for you. You want the best for your child. You should want the best for yourself, too. This may be the way to get it.

Essential points

- Single parents are entitled to financial help and benefits and you should get the help that's available.
- You can claim some benefits even if you are working – Working Families Tax Credit will boost your earnings and Childcare Tax Credit will help with childcare costs.
- You can apply for benefits through your local Jobcentre Plus.
- An adviser can help you do a 'better off' calculation, working out what you might gain and what you might lose by taking a job or further training.
- The New Deal for Lone Parents (NDLP) can help you get back to work if you have taken a break to care for your children.

What if you've got into debt?

Lone parents can suffer a fall in income of about £20 per week when they separate from their partner. One study found that almost half of single parent families had been in arrears in the previous year. Loss of income, low incomes and increased or unexpected expenses are the key reasons lone parents give for their debts.

If you owe money and can't pay it, you may be feeling ashamed and guilty and are reluctant to ask for help. Most people have money problems at some time – the trick is to ask for help and use it. There are several places you can go to talk to a debt counsellor or debt management adviser. They can help you to:

- Get the people who are chasing you for money to give you some time to pay. A debt counsellor can help you talk to the people you owe money to. Find one through the Citizens Advice Bureau (CAB) – see Taking it further for details.

Your debtors want their money, but they are usually reasonable about it *if* you get in touch. If you talk to them they are likely to let you pay a small amount weekly.

- Look at your debts. Sometimes bills may be wrong or unfair. A debt counsellor will help you challenge a charge if it's not right.
- Get help with payments. You may be able to increase your benefits, get loans or grants or seek work to raise the money.
- Pay what you owe. You may need to sit down and work out how you're going to pay off your debts. A debt counsellor could help you sort out which payments can't wait, which can be delayed and how to manage that, and which ones in special circumstances might be set aside.
- Make your money go further in the future. A debt counsellor can help you sort out your spending. It often helps to have someone to talk to for you to see a way to manage.

What about borrowing money to pay debts?

If you need money, be very careful about where you borrow it. Some loans, store cards or credit cards will charge you so much in interest that you end up paying many times more than the original sum you borrowed. A consolidated debt – where you borrow one amount to pay off all your debts and have one debt in one place – may look like a good deal because the amount you pay each week or month may be small, but the number of weeks (or months, or years) you pay the small amount can get hidden in the small print and the actual amount you end up paying is far more than the original debt. If you need money, ask Jobcentre Plus for a grant or a loan or ask CAB for advice on getting a fair loan.

Drawing up a budget

Every family needs to budget but single parent families need to do so even more. However alien or boring or silly it may seem, particularly if you have managed for years without having to do this, it may be worthwhile drawing up a budget to give yourself a picture of how you are going to manage.

Use this template to write down all the money that comes into your family every week, and all the money that goes out. Writing it down allows you to take stock and to manage your finances with less of a shock than suddenly realizing your family may be costing you more than you imagined. When you write it down you don't forget anything and you can spot expenses you might be able to cut down.

Income	Amount	Outgoings	Amount
Income after tax		Rent/mortgage	
Maintenance		Council tax	
Income support		Water rates	
Jobseekers allowance		Electricity/Gas/ Other fuel	
Housing/Council tax benefits		Car: payment for, insurance, tax, petrol	
Working families' tax credit/Childcare tax credit		Travel	
Children's tax credit		Food & household items	
Child benefit		TV licence/rental/ satellite package	
Other		Phone/internet etc.	
		Child care	
		Clothing/shoes	
		Hair cuts	
		Launderette/cleaning	
		Cigarettes	
		Alcohol	
		Papers/magazines	
		CDs, DVDs, downloads etc.	
		Christmas and holidays	
		Gifts: birthdays etc.	
		Entertainment/going out	
		Debt: credit cards, store cards, etc.	
		Savings account payments	
		Other	
Total Income		Total Outgoings	

When you write down and look at what you've got and where it has to go, there may be less temptation to overspend. Lone parents often feel under pressure to spend too much on special times such as holidays and festivals 'to make up for' the losses and hurts involved in being in their particular circumstances. When you can see exactly what you've got, it's a good incentive to think about cutting costs. You might consider:

- banning trips to fast food outlets – bad for your waistline but also very expensive
- cutting down on convenience, pre-packaged food – fresh made is cheaper
- using charity shops for clothes
- shopping with friends to make use of 2 for 1 deals
- buying own brands rather than premium brands
- finding out about free or cheap activities for your family in your area
- walking to save travel costs (and gym fees)
- stopping smoking.

Writing down your budget is also an incentive to spread the load. This could mean sharing cheap or free days out with friends and family to have lots of fun with little expense – going to the park, for a picnic, to the coast rather than pricey trips to theme parks. Children may ask for the latter but love the former even more. Or it could mean sharing the load by involving the kids in budget decisions.

Should you involve children in setting and maintaining a budget?

One enormous benefit of writing this all down is that you can show it to and talk it through with your children. Children need to understand from quite an early age that money is not inexhaustible. If they are in contact with the other parent, money may be being used by you and the other parent to compensate for losses in a child's life. Because they've had such a hard time, both parents may be lenient about requests or demands for certain items, hoping that a new pair of trainers, a visit to a music festival or a new bike may in some way make up for the difficulties of the situation. It does not – and children may find themselves in a cycle where they keep asking for things both because they know they can and because they think it will make them feel better. When it does not do so, they just ask for more.

Children most certainly must not be made to feel responsible if there are financial difficulties, but it is an important learning experience for them to see that the bank of Mum or Dad has its limits. Children can be surprisingly mature and responsible when they can see how much is coming in, and how much is already earmarked. It's the best way to deal with those constant requests.

From the postbag

Since my divorce, I've been working part-time and because my ex makes getting money from him a real trial, I'm struggling. I was thinking about taking one of those 'put all your debts in one place' deals since the amount I have to pay each month is getting bigger and bigger. My biggest problem is shopping. The kids moan and whine if they don't get the food they want – pizza and fizzy drinks seem to make up such a large part of the budget. And don't get me started on clothes – it has to be designer, and a new thing every week, or there's hell to pay. Any suggestions?

It does help to consider what the demands are all about. Having the same routines and especially the same food as ever could be their coping mechanism to keep the hurt and frustrations of the break-up under some sort of control. Demanding constant treats could be a way of asking 'Do you still love me? Will you still be there for me?' – something past experience has told them to doubt since one of their parents may appear to them to have said 'No'.

The best way to tackle it may be to deal with it head on. Show them the budget, reassure them that feeding them healthier and cheaper food and either cutting back on the fizzy drinks or going for own brands does not mean you don't love them. The sad fact is that times have changed and however hard that may be, you have to change some routines to manage the new situation. By going through the budget you can give them choices – and having choices means control, and having some control over their lives is what this is about. If they can see you have only so much money to buy so many things, they can choose – pizza this week or a branded drink next? And challenge them – make a game of doing a blind tasting and see if any of you can tell the difference. As for consolidating your loans – see a financial adviser at the Citizens Advice Bureau. Chances are it's a really bad deal that will cost you far more in the long run. There are other ways to deal with your borrowing. Good luck!

Giving children pocket money, or should it be an allowance?

Having given children a glimpse into what you have to think about when balancing what comes in and what goes out, it might be a good idea to talk with them about how they, too, can learn to manage their own money. Some children are given pocket money – a small amount each week to spend on whatever they choose. Some are allowed to earn extra cash by doing work around the house that does not come under the heading of 'chores' – such as cleaning cars or mowing lawns. Purchases not covered by either pocket money, earnings or gifts may be negotiated separately. In other families, children are given a steadily increasing allowance, and made responsible for certain purchases themselves.

How liberal parents are with the amount of money they give as pocket money and the amount they are prepared to spend on things such as computer games, designer clothes and entertainment may have more to do with their feelings of guilt or difficulty in drawing boundaries than the amount of money coming in. Particularly in lone parent families, it may be important for children to have some unrestricted money of their own to spend on what they like. Having some exercise of choice (thus a feeling of control) will be important to all children, but particularly to those who know the loss of power that can be felt in family upheaval. But, equally, it is really important for children to learn to live within a budget and to recognize that in the real world to have money you need to offer something in exchange, and that the family purse is not bottomless.

Negotiating an allowance

Allowances can be set from quite a young age. You will need to:

- Work out what is spent specifically on the child, apart from household expenses. You might include their out-of-school clothes, entertainment such as games consoles and sports equipment, trips to the cinema and other outings with friends, travel, snacks out, and so on.
- Agree which items the child will be responsible for. Talk this through with the child and vary it depending on their age. Agree increases in the amount and the number of responsibilities as they get older.
- Agree how often to pay the allowance. You might total up an annual amount and then pay it weekly or monthly (which

might mean they would need to save more to allow for larger purchases out of the averaged amount) or quarterly (which would mean they would have to resist spending a large amount at once).

- Agree with the child's other parent, if in contact, whether you will pay all the allowance using child maintenance, or whether one parent will pay most and the other will top up. Make a clear undertaking that only the agreed amount will be paid and you will discuss any other request together so as not to undermine each other.
- Keep the limits! Make it very clear to the child that when money is spent you will not issue more until the next payday. If they blow the whole clothes allowance on one item, or spend all their travel costs, it's their lookout if they grow out of clothes or have to walk to friend's houses before the next payment.

Giving an allowance helps children to learn how to set aside money for things they need or want, and to learn the difference. It helps them learn how to prioritize and pace themselves. They won't learn these essential skills if you bail them out if they make a mistake. All financial disasters are learning experiences. Far better to have to cope with a misspent allowance, when they still eat and sleep under a secure roof and have clothes to wear (even if not the latest thing), than discover they can't manage a budget when they're adults, out in the world by themselves.

But more important is that children in single parent families often need to flex their muscles around responsibility and control, and giving them control and responsibility for their own cash from an early age can do this. Children (and parents) in single parent families need to understand the meanings we attach to money and how money can be manipulated to control or worry others. By making the issue a debate you can manage the problematical potential of money and help all of you to function better.

Summary

- Children are the financial responsibility of both parents, whether they live together or apart.
- Money has a significance beyond the ability to pay bills. Money can be used to control or manipulate, bribe or punish. It's important to separate emotional issues from financial ones when managing your finances.

- The calculation and the payment of maintenance are best done by voluntary agreement. Asking for the advice of a sympathetic solicitor can be useful. In cases where such an agreement is impractical, help can be sought from the courts, a solicitor or the Child Maintenance and Enforcement Commission (CMEC).

- You are entitled to help if money is scarce. The Department for Work and Pensions (DWP) is the UK government department that deals with benefits.

- Jobcentre Plus, Citizen's Advice Bureau (CAB) or One Parent Families can help you work out your 'better off' decision when looking at going back to work.

- CAB, Jobcentre Plus and debt counsellors can also help you with advice and support about debt and borrowing.

- Drawing up a carefully considered budget can be an enormous help in controlling your and your child's money needs and concerns.

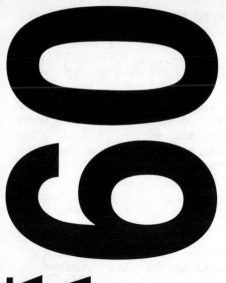

09

widening your horizons

In this chapter you will learn:

- why friends and a social network are so important
- how to get your new state into perspective
- how families, on both sides, can be important as friends and as sources of help
- how to find and make new friends for yourself and your children
- how to find friends safely on the internet
- how being on your own can be better than being half of an unhappy couple
- how to manage holidays as a single parent.

Making friends and socializing

Everyone loves a lover but it's amazing how friends may melt away once you become single. Most couples who separate find their friends fall into three camps – mine, yours and neither of ours.

Some of your friends may tend towards supporting you, some your ex-partner. You may think it might have something to do with what precipitated the break, with people backing the person they see as the 'innocent party'. In fact, support often has far more to do with the strength or type of bonds before the split than what happened around it.

Shared friends

In most relationships it is the woman who cultivates and facilitates friendships – making arrangements to meet and stoking the emotional fires and thus the links between families. And, of course, many friendships are between couples who have children at around the same time or based around child-related activities. So it's obvious that when there is a break-up many couples and their families will stand by the person with the primary care of the children. But even if you have been horribly wronged and abused, even if you have been left with children to care for and a real need for friendships to carry you through, you may sadly discover that the friends you thought you had fade away as soon as your lone state is an openly acknowledged issue. Before assuming it's your fault or something you'll have to accept, explore why some people might let you down as soon as you really need them.

In some circumstances, it's because there is a general assumption that you need to be part of a twosome to join in. Couples go out for drinks together and meals round a table are seen as shared by equal numbers of men and women. Some of your friends may feel awkward breaking that traditional pattern, or may even take for granted that you'd feel the odd one out if they asked you too.

Some friendships fade because there was a special interest in one member of the relationship, and the friendship goes with the person who held the interest. So you may find that although you and a partner spent a lot of time with a particular couple and you'd imagine you'd still see them, because their original link was with your partner, they stay in touch with him/her and you lose out. Very few friends will remain in touch with both members of a split relationship. People feel caught in the middle, having to support one or the other – either because they have lost sympathy for one partner, or simply because they feel unable to balance being even-handed and objective with both. But both separating parents may find certain friends lose touch, whatever the reasons or circumstances of the break-up and whatever the nature of the friendship beforehand.

Why do some friends avoid lone parents?

One reason for this is a fear that your single state may be 'catching'. Even stable couples may shy away from asking a newly separated friend over in case their single status gives their partner ideas. And when there are already cracks or doubts in a relationship, both members may be highly reluctant to have contact with someone who can be living proof that two can become one, and quicker than you might think. They may be frightened you'd give their partner pointers on how it's done and why they might take the initiative. They may fear that since you're on the loose, you might also be on the lookout for a new partner, and make a play for theirs. Or that a partner capable or prone to being unfaithful may see you as an easy opportunity.

This is as true when the reason for your being on your own is bereavement as it is after separation. Illness and death are also, superstitiously, seen as infectious and that being with you may pass on the bad luck. Friends may avoid you after the loss of a partner because they simply don't know what to say, whether the other partner has left or died. They may fear they cannot handle your grief or anger or know what to say, and that the easiest option is simply to avoid it.

If you're a single mother, some friends with whom you've always shared childcare or seen when your children play together may suddenly be fine to go on seeing you for after-school weekday play dates, but make excuses if you suggest something over the weekend. Playtime when it's just you and them may be safe – events when their other partner is there too may not be seen as acceptable. They may feel they are being sensitive to your situation because their partner's presence may be a hurtful reminder that they still have a partner and you do not. Or, unfairly, that you may be a threat to their relationship. Sometimes, the reason they shy away is that they (unfairly) feel they're a family and you're not and weekends are 'family time'.

Single parent dads may have an even worse time as ranks close against them with women either warned off by their partners, or feeling awkward and defensive.

You yourself may find the prospect of making efforts with old friends unappealing. They could remind you, uncomfortably, of the times when you were all partnered, and seeing them just rubs salt in the wound of your separation. Sometimes, you may find that you have drawn away from people you knew during the run up to your separation anyway. In some couples, one partner, deliberately or without realizing it, may have isolated their partner and put a barrier between them and friends who might have helped while the relationship was foundering. Or you might have avoided friends, perhaps because you felt so miserable or confused and didn't want to share it with them. They may feel guilty at having left you alone and you may feel hesitant at going back to them.

This avoidance of families to whom a loss has occurred can be particularly painful and confusing for children. They may find the parents of some of their friends put barriers in their way and discourage friendships that may be important and longstanding.

Why are friends and social networks so important?

You may feel dispirited and tempted to give up, retreating back into a lonely existence, just you, your children and your family. Resist this urge. Your support networks are really important. You need friends to give you reassurance and time for yourself, to help you see you are an individual as well as a parent. You can't be 'the parent' all the time – you need the chance to let off steam and be yourself as an individual. You need friends to put your situation in perspective and to help you in the very important job of caring for and bringing up your kids. You need friends so your children have time with other adults, and their children. And of course, they need friends of their own to have fun with.

It's worth making the effort to rekindle old friendships and to make new ones. And if you were lucky enough to have some friends who stood by you and supported you in just the way you needed, with unconditional affection and loyalty but with respect to the needs of your children in not having their other parent criticized, you'll want to strengthen and continue those bonds.

You may not be able to change other people's behaviour or beliefs, but you can do something about your own. The more pride and self confidence you have, the more other people will accept you for who you are and forget the ridiculous reservations they may have had about having you as part of their social network.

How to get your family shape into perspective

Being a lone parent may be difficult and hard work but in essence it's no different from being in any other family. Families come in all shapes and sizes. They always have but up to the last century there was social stigma attached to having a family that does not conform to the 'two adults of the opposite sex living with and bringing up their own children' model. If you were a single person past a certain age you were looked down on, if you were a couple on your own with no children you were treated with sympathy, even if that was your choice, and if you were a parent on your own you were avoided. Today what constitutes a 'family' is being redefined. Plenty of people are remaining single by choice, and showing that it is a lifestyle they enjoy. Similarly, even if your situation has been forced upon you by the actions of your ex partner, you can see a positive side to the shape of your family now. Being on your own is infinitely preferable to being half of a warring, unhappy couple. Being a parent on your own is infinitely better for your children than their having two miserable parents.

Sit down with paper and pen and draw up two columns, headed 'Good Things' and 'Bad Things'. Start with the 'Bad Things' and list all the downsides of being on your own. You may put down things like:

- losing some friends
- not being able to go to parties
- having no one to read the Sunday papers with in bed
- having to manage your children on your own in the supermarket
- having no-one to talk to about the kids.

Then start listing 'Good Things'. You may find you come up with:

- realizing who your true friends are
- finding out how helpful people can be
- enjoying being with your children with less conflict
- finding your own way of negotiating with your kids
- sharing worries and finding reassurance from people who listen to you.

A lot of the time, all it takes is a change in your perspective rather than a change in what is actually going on. It's that old 'is the glass half full or half empty?' thing. Whatever your natural tendency, you can make yourself begin to see it as half full rather than half empty, and once you start you can go on seeing it that way. Once you can focus on the upsides rather than the downsides, you can not only manage the situation but thrive in it, as can your children. But just as important, your positive attitude rubs off on other people and has them accepting you for who and what you are.

Family can be important too

Your family can be key in making a new social life on your own. Family, after all, may have their own doubts and anxieties about the relationship break-up and may have their own feelings and allegiances that could be less than helpful. You may have to be quite firm with family members who feel the best thing they can do for you is to be totally on your side, and see that as meaning they have to be critical and hostile towards your ex-partner. This, as we've seen, can make your children unhappy. But more often family loyalty can be enormously helpful, and should be utilized. Your parents – your children's grandparents – are likely to be helpful and supportive, offering care so you can have some time off as well as shared time with them so you can enjoy your children together. You may also find the other grandparents – your ex-partner's parents – can be as welcoming and as helpful.

Needing alternative social contacts may also enable you to find that other people in your family, who you may have occasionally encountered at large family gatherings, are actually friends in waiting; cousins, nieces and nephews, uncles and aunts. All may have families of around the same age as your children, or of an age or with similar interests and tastes as you.

Being on your own can be the impetus to get in touch and see if you can widen your circle and have some fun with them. With family, you have half the work of 'getting to know you' done, and don't really need an excuse to say 'Shall we meet up?'

Essential points

- Some friends may stop getting in touch with you once you are a single parent. They may fear that your state is catching, or that you could be a threat to their relationship.
- Keeping or making a new network of friends is really important for you and your children.
- It's important to get your family shape into perspective. Being a single parent family may be difficult but it's no different from any other family.
- Being on your own is infinitely preferable to being half of a warring, unhappy couple. Being a parent on your own is infinitely better for your children than them having two miserable parents.
- Your family can be as important as your friends in keeping your social life active.

If you do feel you have a full circle of friends and need look no further, then enjoy them. It's always worth recognizing that all social contacts, whether romantic, friendly or with family, need tending. One of the reasons for any of these relationships foundering or failing is that we take them for granted. Whether it's a parent or a close friend, an acquaintance or a love interest, we should always take the time to call or text or meet for coffee, to keep the lines of communication going. And it's also worth recognizing that people you know and keep up with often give you opportunities to meet others. Even when you have some issues and don't see eye to eye, it's a good idea to keep in touch, as new contacts may emerge if you do.

A cup of coffee with a friend

Imagine you have a very large jam or honey jar – one that takes at least a litre. Fill it to the top with golf balls. It would be full, wouldn't it?

Ah, but now imagine pouring in a few handfuls of small stones or gravel, shaking the jar as you do so. The stones would fill the open areas between the golf balls. Is it full then?

You'd probably say yes. Except, now imagine pouring in a bag of sand, again shaking it as you do so, so the sand fills up all the remaining nooks and crannies. Is the jar now full?

Maybe. Now imagine taking two cups of coffee and pouring them into the jar. Try it – you'll find the liquid finds spaces you didn't think were there.

So what's all this about? Well, the jam jar is your life. The golf balls are the important things – your family, your children, your health, your friends, and the things you really like doing – the things you really need and that really matter. The things that, if all else was gone, you'd still value and know made life worth living.

The stones are the other things that matter such as your job, your home, your favourite belongings, perhaps your car. The sand is everything else – the small stuff: keeping up with the neighbours, having the latest fashions, doing the housework.

If you put the sand in the jar first, there would be no room for the golf balls or the stones. If you put the stones in first, there would still be room for the sand but no room for the golf balls.

If you spend all your time and energy on the small stuff – whether your house is dusted, whether you have the latest clothes to wear – you have no room for the things that are of real value. If you concentrate on your job or your car or home, you don't give the time and effort you could and should on the issues that really matter – your children, your family, your own health.

The moral of this tale is to pay attention to the things that are really critical to your and your children's happiness. Play with them, rather than worrying about how tidy their bedrooms are. Make the effort to eat healthily and do exercise. See your family and friends as often as you can. Take care of the golf balls first, the things that really matter, and then look to the stones and ignore the sand.

And the coffee? Well, you need to recognize, with all those golf balls and stones and sand, that you can always find room for a coffee with a friend.

Where can you meet new friends?

One of the problems of starting again, either because some of your old friends have dropped off, because you have relied on your partner for all your socializing, or because you have moved, is that finding and making friends may be a skill that you have forgotten. It is, after all, something we tend to associate with being a teenager or in your twenties. We find friends at school, at college or at work. If you're long past the first two and either not at work or working in a small team, you could be forgiven for wondering 'So where do I find friends?'

How to find friends through your children

You can find many people of like minds and similar situations through groups that cater for your kids. You have the opportunity to speak with and get to know other parents if you use childcare and see them when you drop off or collect, or if you stay. You can also meet other parents at the school gates. Other places to meeet parents include:

- Supervised play areas or adventure playgrounds – your local library can tell you where the nearest ones are.
- Local events – look in shop windows, on community or supermarket notice boards or in the local press for news on any child and parent-friendly events.
- Museums – look out for parents like yourself or suggest to people that you meet to have a day out there and share the fun and the work. Ask your local library for what's available in your area.
- Parks – some have small zoos or petting corners, playgrounds and activities, where children can have fun and you can meet other parents. Ask at your local library. Small children would also enjoy a visit to a city farm. These are real farms, in towns, and there are many all over the country. For details see Taking it further.
- Leisure and sporting activities for your children – ask the school or your local library about tennis, climbing, skiing or swimming clubs and go along to watch, and chat to other parents.
- Gingerbread (now incorporated with One Parent Families) and Parentline both run and know about family fun events, in term time or holidays. See Taking it further for contact details.

How to find friends online

Virtual friends are no substitute for real-life friends, but can be enormously useful. They can be there for you when you can't get out and your friends aren't available. They're also a good stepping stone, if you've lost confidence and need to establish the skill of making friends and chatting to people, in a safe and arm's length way. Joining online communities can help you discuss issues you might have felt uncomfortable raising face to face. There are quite a few online communities for parents. Try:

- the message boards at Parentline Plus, which includes one for lone parents
- the forums at Single Parent Action Network – SPAN
- the message boards at UK Parents Lounge, which has online forums for parents and one specifically for single parents
- the community at Parents.com, which includes a single mums forum.
- the online forums at Dad.info, the website run by Fathers Direct
- the online forums at HomeDad or Single Fathers.

If you aren't online at home you can use a computer at your local library to do this. If you're going online, pay attention to the advice on safe surfing and be careful if you decide to meet anyone who you have talked with on a website.

Rules for safe internet use

Always keep these common sense rules about safe internet use:

- If you're communicating with anyone you don't already know in the real world, don't tell them anything that could let them contact you offline. Keep your home address and telephone number to yourself. Use an online name that doesn't reveal your real name or where you come from. Be careful to whom you reveal family details.
- Don't forget that in cyberspace, no one can see you. That nice parent, just like you, can in reality be someone out to exploit you.
- Be careful about agreeing to a face to face meeting with another user. If you do arrange one, insist on it being in a public place, preferably somewhere you are known, and take a mobile phone, with a friend on standby on a one-button number. Or, better still, take a friend along either to join you or be at a nearby table. Yes, even if you're expecting to meet a woman.

- Don't get into 'flame wars' – angry and abusive exchanges. Never respond to messages or chat that you find hostile, threatening, or inappropriate. Report such exchanges to the webmaster of the site. Some parent communities make a point of being 'robust' so be prepared.
- Remember that everything you read online may not be true. If it seems 'too good to be true', it probably is. Be very careful about any offers that involve you going to a meeting, or having someone visit your house, or that involve you giving information about yourself.

How to find friends for yourself

You can also find friends for yourself at a wide range of social events and opportunities. Look out for:

- Special interest clubs – salsa dancing, rambling, wine tasting, amateur dramatics, art appreciation. It doesn't have to be something you know anything about, just something you think you'd want to learn about and may involve people you'd like. Look for them on notice boards, at your local library or arts or community or leisure centre, or in your local newspaper.
- Lifelong learning opportunities – do a course in parenting, pottery, tai chi, French, cooking, mechanics. Anything you think might be fun, and again might have members you'd get on with. Ask at your local library or your child's school.
- Make it clear to friends, family, fellow workers that you're happy to accept invitations to events with them. Sometimes people don't ask only because they think you're too busy to join them.
- Join a gym or exercise class. This can be a pricey option but one that might do you an enormous amount of good, not only by improving your health and fitness but in making the point to yourself and others that you deserve and need looking after, too. And it may give you the chance to meet new friends.
- If you see other parents regularly meeting in places like coffee shops, go there too. Make eye contact and smile or respond to an open remark. If you're seen often enough the nod and smile will become an invitation to join in.

Don't forget, you're simply looking for like-minded people with whom to pass the time of day and share a few thoughts, a few ideas and maybe coffee. Charge in looking for best friends with whom to share the holiday of a lifetime tomorrow and you'll scare them off. It's easy when you've been in a partnership for some time and then had to go through loss and pain to lose the knack of making friends and opening communication. Some tips that it would help to keep in mind are:

- People can't read your mind. They don't know that you're wanting to be friendly or are scared stiff. You have to be open and honest for them to realize you'd like to be friends.
- Body language says far more than words. Sit hunched up, with your eyes lowered and your arms crossed, and you may as well be wearing a sign saying 'GO AWAY!' If you want to make friends, sit up, meet eyes and smile.
- You don't have to say much to open a conversation. A remark about the weather or the coffee or what's in the paper will do it.
- Being a good listener is often more important than being a good talker. Ask an open question – one that can't be answered simply by yes, no or maybe – then listen and respond.
- Give of yourself. This doesn't mean tell everyone your deepest secrets at once. It simply means be yourself.
- Share as much about yourself and your opinions and life as they do, so you are evenly matched.

From the postbag

I used to meet two friends every Saturday for coffee when we'd done our supermarket shopping but since I divorced they've both made excuses and no longer come. There are some other mums at a café I go to and I know a couple of them are single mums too. But they're not very friendly. They smile and say hello but they never ask me to join them. How can I make friends?

Don't wait to be asked. Your 'body language' says as much as your words when you meet people. I suspect yours is saying 'I'm fine as I am, thank you very much.' If they've seen you with other people they may assume you're on your own by choice. And if you sit hunched up, turned or just looking away people leave you alone. They don't ask you to join in because they think you're the one being unfriendly or don't need them. They don't know you're shy or scared and have been let down by your former friends. Next time, take a deep breath and go over. Look someone in the eyes and just make some remark about your child or theirs – a compliment, a question, a comment. It may lead to a chat. Or it may just break the ice so next time you can smile and say hello, and take it from there. It's scary and takes effort to make friends, I know. But it's worth risking being turned away because the chances are you'll be welcomed in. Good luck!

What things could we do as a single family to help our social networks?

There are plenty of things you and your children can do to keep you occupied and entertained on weekends and during holidays. Some of these things have the added benefit of drawing you and other people together and helping to either make or cement those social networks. Try some of these:

- Ask your children to produce a newsletter. Model it on their favourite magazine, with top stories (like 'Smashing secrets of our sizzling summer fun' or 'Daring escape by hamster!') and features (like 'How we kept warm this winter'). They could include interviews, cartoons, recipes, horoscopes, pictures – everything to report what they've been doing or would like to do. Then help them send it to relatives and friends, asking for feedback, and saying they intend to produce one for each holiday period.

- Set up a family blog, get all your children to contribute and invite friends and family to view it.

- Have a listen to the message on the answer machine on your phone. Is it boring? Did you record it, does it only represent you? Let your kids record a new one, with sound effects, music, drama and soul. They can make a whole production number of it – who knows, you may unleash a budding screenwriter and director – and anyone ringing you can have a good laugh as well as be more inclined to leave a message.

- Suggest that all of you sit down and write a letter to someone – a relative or a friend. Getting in touch passes a spare hour and, more importantly, it fosters links and may lead to invitations and contact.

- Practise talking to people about anything, anytime. Take some slips of paper and on each write a question such as 'How can you cheer up someone who is sad?' or 'If you could be anyone for a day, who would it be and why?' Put them in a jar and while you're having a family meal, or are together in the evening, each of you pull out a question and see what ideas everyone comes up with.

- Take your children to your local travel agent, tourist bureau and library and get brochures, maps and books. Get them to come up with a travel plan for their dream holiday. Then, ideas storm how you might put some of the elements they particularly liked into reality. Think about sharing travel and accommodation with other single parents or friends.

This gives the kids someone to play with and you and the other adults someone with whom to enjoy a break and share childcare.

- Are your children fascinated by firemen, policemen, butchers, bakers or candlestick makers? Ring up your local shop or station, tell the manager or supervisor that you have a youngster who thinks what they do is super cool and ask if there is any chance of an informal tour. Nine times out of ten, you'll be welcomed with open arms. Ask your children's friends parents if they'd like to come too.

- Support a child's request to have a sleepover. They take time and effort and are exhausting but they foster good friendships. Ideas storm the rules – you may want to insist as non-negotiable that you may stroll in at any time to check they're okay, and agree that food should not be too fat-, sugar- or caffeine-laden (and no alcohol) and that you'll vet films or games to make sure they're age appropriate. Then accept that a sleepover is nothing of the sort since they'll be up all night playing or talking or watching and will sleep all day afterwards, but be very happy!

Essential points

- It may feel difficult to find new friends once you are beyond school or college and if you don't work in a place with a wide range of colleagues.
- You can meet new contacts through your children, online or at many special interest clubs or local venues.
- You need to make an effort to be social, welcoming and friendly if you want to meet new people.
- You and your children can do a lot to make and keep links with friends and family and to practise the skills of getting on with other people.

How to manage holidays as a single parent

Holidays are probably the most difficult areas to negotiate as a single parent but with a bit of research and planning you can find something to please yourself and your children.

- Investigate what deals your local travel agent offers. Some holiday companies have woken up to the fact that there is a niche market there and will now offer package holidays with an eye to satisfying the needs and tastes of single parent families, without the extra expense loaded on because it's one adult rather than two.

- Contact One Parent Families (see Taking it further) to see what ideas they have for single parent family holidays.

- Ask around your friends and relatives to see if you can arrange a holiday in a gîte or a villa with several families. Several adults and a group of children often means that you can take full advantage of family tickets, both when travelling and when there. You can also share out childcare tasks so all of you have some time doing your own thing and some time having fun with the kids.

- Swap houses with a friend or relative for a few days. You could do it with a contact abroad or at the other end of the country if you have one, but even changing houses a few streets away gives you a fresh outlook and a break.

- If money is tight, research what is available in youth hostels and camp sites. You may find the idea basic, your kids may see it as an adventure second to none.

- If you can't afford to go away but have a garden, declare the house off-limits and pitch a tent in your own garden. If you don't have a tent, drape a sheet over a clothesline for shelter and pile sleeping bags or bedding inside. Invite your friends who have children a similar age to yours and make it a major camp-out. Cook on a barbecue, tell stories and sing songs and see who can find the Big Dipper and Orion's Belt.

- Consider taking a holiday with the child's other parent, and their family if they have re-partnered. Sounds terrible? Your children may love it as a chance to see both their parents in relaxed surroundings and it would give you and the other family a chance to build bridges. It would let you have time off doing your own thing – each parent takes half the responsibility for childcare. You could all be part of a larger villa party if you wanted to dilute the face-to-face time between the two of you.

Summary

- Friends can disappear after your separation. Rebuilding friendships and developing a strong social network for yourself and your children are a priority.
- Some friends desert because of their own anxieties, not because of any failings by you.
- Getting back your self-esteem and confidence can help you recognize that being a single parent is really no different from being in any other family form.
- There are many ways of finding new friends for yourself and your children, including relatively new ways like the internet. You should explore every possible avenue in your search.
- Family holidays may need more planning when you're a single parent but are just as much fun as ever.

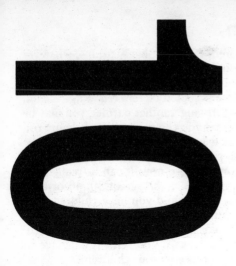

10

new partners – dating and mating

In this chapter you will learn:
- why learning to date again can seem so daunting
- how to deal with the changes in your life
- how to look for a new partner and increase your social network
- how to begin again and decide what sort of relationship you should be looking for
- how children may react when a new person comes along and what to tell them
- the precautions you need to take when you begin to date again.

Beginning again

You're a parent with children, which probably means, whatever your actual age, that you have fairly dim memories of the dubious joys of dating – the excitement and anticipation, the anxiety of whether you'll be accepted or rejected. Single again, and possibly contemplating finding another partner, you may be looking back and wondering if you can manage it all again. You may remember how easy it was, and are concerned it won't be so this time round. Maybe you remember how hard it was, and are convinced it will be even more so now. It can be really hard to step back into the dating scene at the age of 30, 40 or even 50, when a relationship has ended and you have children. You may have forgotten how to flirt, how to get to know someone, how to ask them out or make it clear you'd like to be asked. Now, you won't only be thinking of yourself. You'll have to balance your own needs with those of your children.

Being a parent is your job and your responsibility and you won't want to jeopardize your children's well-being for selfish ends. But sometimes 'being selfish' is a good thing. You have rights and reasonable needs, too. You have a responsibility to look after yourself – an unhappy, lonely person who isn't getting their own needs met will find it hard to give their children all the emotional support they need. So, although as a single parent you cannot approach dating as if you were a single, you should still see it as something you want to do and should do.

Why is the thought of dating again so daunting?

Meeting people and building relationships are skills. You might have lost these skills while you were in your previous relationship, or during the period you have been a parent on your own. And while the first time around you might have been scared, confused and sensitive to criticism, second time around you may find yourself feeling all that plus all sorts of different anxieties.

Your self-esteem and self-confidence may have already taken a battering. However your previous relationship ended, the chances are you may be feeling rejected or abandoned or in mourning. You may be low in feelings of self-worth. The last thing you need is to believe that as well as failing in the last relationship, you could now fail in getting a new one going. Just as when you were a teenager, you may look around you and see other people appearing so confident and skilled in the way they manage their relationships, leaving you feeling unskilled and entirely lacking in self-assurance.

The reality is that it's never easy to find a new partner, whether at 16 or 60. One reason is that the ability to attract other people to you and to get on with them is a skill. And skills need to be gained and then have to be practised to be kept. The facilities for feeling confident in asking someone out, getting to know them, negotiating what sort of relationship you're going to have and how much, how soon are gained through experience. It's a case of use them or lose them. Second timers are often appalled and frightened to discover how much they've forgotten, and how false it all feels when they try to date again.

How are the skills of dating and being with a partner different?

While you're in a settled relationship, you learn and use other skills. You and your partner build up the ability to be intimate, to get close, to create the shorthand that lovers have with each other, to use the knowledge you have about each other. You learn to rely on that closeness, and this reliance can leave you feeling highly uncertain with a new person. You may find yourself making assumptions about a new partner, expecting them to do something, say something, like or appreciate something, and be taken by surprise when they don't react as you expected. The problem may be that you're running on tramlines set by your previous relationship, and forgetting that this is someone else, someone different. It's not just about the slip of the tongue that has you call them by another name. It's also about the shock of surprise when you expect them to like a certain film or a certain food, and find they don't.

So what should you do? You need to get back in the saddle – but remember that you may need some time to re-learn how. It's a process, and you may need to take it one step at a time. Remind yourself that sometimes you have to take one step forward and two steps back. Eventually it will become two steps forward for every step back.

- Give yourself time to finish and mourn your last relationship. Unfinished business from the past can spoil an otherwise wonderful new romance.
- Take some time to reflect on what went wrong last time. It's very common to follow patterns when looking for romantic partners. You may have fallen for a person, or fallen into a type

of relationship, that does you harm. And unless and until you can identify what happened and why, you may simply replace one for another, with a similar result. It may have all been down to your ex – but *you* chose that person. You may need to consider the choices you make in order not to do so again.

- Remind yourself that dating and romancing are skills you may need to brush up on, and that anyone will be rusty if they've been away from the scene for a time. Remember what it was like and practise those skills, with friends or even children. Practise asking questions to get conversation going, listening and learning and acknowledging.

- Recognize that a new partner is not your old one, born-again. You'll need to establish and develop your own jokes, references and knowledge of each other between you.

- Accept that you may be older and wiser a second time around, but that you'll be starting off as fresh as any teenager. You need to allow yourself to be less than perfect in the skills of flirting, getting on and even getting it on with a new partner.

- Reflect that one advantage of being mature may be the ability to forgive yourself mistakes and laugh at misunderstandings. Unlike first-timers, you do at least know that the world won't end if you lose out or lose face.

- Rejoice that love can be as powerful, overwhelming and exciting to a 60-year-old as it is to a 16-year-old. It may seem hard to be on the roundabout looking for a partner again. The incentive is that once you find the right person it will be well worth it.

How to cope with change and with 'pinch points'

It's helpful to remind yourself of two things when looking at your new life after separation.

1 You don't go from one life to another in a one quick leap, nor do you adjust overnight. You'll have a series of fits and starts, of advances and retreats. How you manage and how you see it will waver from old perspectives and old habits, to new ones, from being upbeat to being in despair. This is nothing to worry about and exactly as you should expect.

2 Your feelings and ability to manage will constantly come up against new challenges. We tend to feel that life proceeds on

a level; once you're unhappy, you stay unhappy and once you're content, you stay so. We feel that if we have difficulty managing a 'normal' experience in life such as having a baby, getting married, having our kids become teenagers, it's because we are incompetent. Or it's because our kids are the problem and uniquely troubled and troublesome children. The truth is that all these and many more are what we call common 'pinch points'.

'Pinch points' are those times in your life when you're up against decisions, feelings and changes, in you and in your family, that are troublesome and involved. Having a new baby, experiencing your kids go through the teenage years, being responsible for family obligations such as marriages and weddings, and death, are all 'pinch points'. They're transitional experiences, when you pass from one stage of your life to another, and perhaps one era is ended and another begun. Every single one of them is difficult to deal with and every single one of us finds it hard to cope with them. So you're actually being perfectly normal in having a hard time. Knowing you're not unusual and having advanced warning that these will be tricky situations and tricky times, can help.

What would help is for you to recognize that:

- change happens
- changes, even good changes, are complicated to deal with.

Change happens

Life is about change. When we were young we looked forward to being an adult and had this idea that once we got there, everything would be static and stable. We'd be happy and stay happy. We'd be in charge and stay in charge. As you've now realized, the Happy Ever After isn't as simple as that. We go on learning and developing and finding new things throughout our life. No sooner do we reach one stage then another comes along. This becomes apparent when we have children, who seem in their early years to change in appearance and competency from day to day.

What may be less obvious is that even adults go through a similar fluidity too. You learn things and look at things differently every day and certainly the person you were last year is not the person you are today. The Greek philosopher Heraclitus put it perfectly when he reflected that no one can step into the same river twice because the river, having flowed on, will not be the same river; and the person, having moved on, will not be the same person. It helps to realize that nothing stands still and that this is the normal state of affairs.

Changes, even good changes, are complicated to deal with

It may be easy to accept that change is difficult to manage when it's a change such as a relationship break-up or a loss of a life you found comfortable. It may be puzzling, however, when you find yourself making heavy weather of something that on one level is positive. If you either chose to leave a relationship that was harming you and your children, or have come to terms with the other person leaving by recognizing that it actually improves your situation, you may then wonder if you have made a mistake if it seems hard to manage. A new home may seem exciting, a new job may appear encouraging but you could be alarmed to discover you struggle with it.

The fact to keep in mind is that all change is a challenge. We don't like being startled out of familiar routines and well-known habits. Everyone, no matter how competent, self-confident and skilled, finds embracing change needs some effort. To manage it, you need to:

- forgive yourself finding it hard – everyone does
- cast your mind back to what you are leaving and acknowledge how much you may miss it
- focus on the change and what it brings to you
- concentrate on the positive aspects of the change and celebrate them.

You may find it helps to sit down with paper and pen and write lists. First draw up two columns. At the top of the page write 'What I'm leaving' and in the two columns write down first all the things you'll regret losing, and then all the things you won't miss. Balance up the two and mourn the first, but be relieved about the second.

Then draw up another two columns. At the top of the page write 'What I'm gaining' and in the two columns write down first all the things you're finding difficult about the change, and then all the things you are benefiting from. Balance up the two and use the first as pointers for things you need to work on, and celebrate all the things in the second.

Finding a new partner

You may have to make determined efforts to find yourself a new partner. Unlike your teenage years when, at school or college, you were surrounded by other young people around the same age and in the same marital state, a lot of your friends are likely to be couples or people who are in the same situation as you. You may not have access to a large pool of people with whom you'd like to make a date. Most of us find partners:

• through school or college
• at work
• through friends or family
• by meeting them at social events
• by getting to know them in our neighbourhood.

When you look at that list you can see that actually only one avenue may not be open to you (and even that may be available, if you take some adult training or education). You may not be back to work yet, or you may work, as so many of us do now, in small teams even in a large organization. But all the other routes are there, just as they ever were. And a few new ones may have opened up too. You can also add:

• social networking on the internet
• dating agencies.

There one more reason to go cautiously in the early days if you are a single mother. The reason being that horrible as it may sound, paedophiles have been known to deliberately target single mothers in order to get close to their children. If you're a single mother, you do need to be extra aware and sensitive to the behaviour of any man who comes into your life who knows you have children, or any man who seems keen to develop your relationship as soon as he learns that fact. That's not to say every man who is keen is a risk; it's simply to draw your attention to a little known but serious fact, for you to consider. If you would like further support, contact the NSPCC (see Taking it further for details).

How to widen your social network

It may seem a terrible cliché, but now really is the time to join clubs and classes, to widen your social network as much as possible. Learn how to maintain your car or speak Italian, dance the tango, cook, write, orienteer. If you can make some time in your schedule, do some voluntary work locally. Go places you'll meet people, or help people and use it to get back your self esteem and to make friends. It can be difficult when you're the only parent your child has at home and so you feel totally responsible, all of the time. Many single parents feel guilty at the idea of going out and enjoying themselves, as if they must make up for what might have happened in their family by staying home 24/7. But you don't do your children any good by denying yourself a life or pleasure. Being a martyr rebounds on them.

• It makes them feel guilty when they realize that you give up what benefits you, for their sake.
• It gives them poor messages about how parents behave – that a parent is always and only a parent with no life of their own.
• It puts a burden on them, to repay you for your denial.
• It can make you tired, frustrated and resentful.

When looking for new contacts, use anything and anyone that comes to hand. It's a fortunate fact of twenty-first-century life that people seem to have outgrown the stigma attached to using dating agencies, and to being honest with friends by being able to say 'Help me meet new people'. You can ask friends and family to introduce you to the people they know, and feel confident in approaching people you know by sight and introducing yourself without it giving you 'a bad reputation' anymore. As long as you use the safety rules outlined in Chapter 09, you can also feel positive about using social network sites on the internet. Use common sense and recognize you sometimes have to risk rejection by making an approach.

From the postbag

I really would like to meet someone to love and marry. I've had a few relationships – if you could call them relationships – since my divorce came through but none that went anywhere. Some men just seemed interested in sex, some were very nice and good fun but not ready to settle down and some were simply way off my wavelength. I seem to have run through all the available men in my immediate vicinity and a friend suggested that I try a dating agency but I'm not sure I'm that desperate yet. What can you suggest?

I don't think you have to be desperate to try a dating or introduction agency, or any other way to meet people. You do, however, need to be careful and very clear about what you want and how to get it. Agencies that simply ask you to fill in a form and computer match you might not get you what you want – you could again find yourself with people only out for sex or not at all your type. Those that offer a personal service are expensive, but it may be worth the expense if it means you find a soul mate.

Decide whether you want a date or a partner, because the agencies that offer matching for people wanting someone who is serious tend to be the ones on the upper expense level. However, they ask more questions and try to give a good level of security to members. Only go to one that is a member of the Association of British Introduction Agencies (see Taking it further for details). Look, perhaps, for one that fits you and your lifestyle – a dining or lunch club or one for special interests so you might meet a range of people in a less pressured situation. Or try a singles holiday. Whatever you do, tell your friends what you are doing and keep the common sense rules. And then go out and enjoy yourself! Good luck!

What should you do when joining an introduction agency or marriage bureau?

- Check that the agency is a member of the ABIA – members have to keep to a strict code of practice.
- Ask how many introductions you are likely to be given.
- Make sure you give as much information as possible and tell the truth! You get out what you put in.
- Don't give up if you don't get the right person at once – it can take time.

- If you're not getting what you want, tell the agency and give them a chance to put it right.

Agencies to avoid
- Those that use a PO box number.
- Those that use a premium rate telephone number.
- Those that are not prepared to give you details of their fees on the phone or in their literature.
- Those that ask for a membership fee without giving you the chance to visit them.

When you go on a date
- Tell someone what you're doing and have their number on speed dial in case you need to call for a lift home.
- Meet in public not at your home or theirs.
- Start casual – meet up for a coffee rather than commit yourself to spending a whole evening with someone you might not click with.
- Do unto others as you would be done by. If you decide you don't want to meet up again, say 'Thanks for a really nice evening. I don't think we're suited for a long-term relationship so I think we'll end it here.' Don't make excuses or say you'll ring with no intention of doing so.
- Be yourself – don't pretend to be someone you're not. But be positive and don't do yourself down.

How to begin again

You need to recognize that going out and opening yourself to the possibility of a new relationship is the best thing you can do.

- Forgive yourself for feeling apprehensive – it's not you, it *is* hard to begin again.
- Take it one step at a time – you won't become the life and soul of the party with a social life the envy of all at a stroke.
- Become self-sufficient – when a new person comes along you should want to be with them because they matter, not because they're the next best thing to being alone.
- Put yourself about – new friends won't come knocking at your door, you have to go and find them.
- Be positive – look at yourself in the mirror every morning and tell yourself you're wonderful. If you believe it, so will everyone else!

How and when should I tell a date I have children?

Start as you mean go on – by letting anyone new in your life know who and what you are. Even if this is to just be casual, your date needs to know you have other people in your life. Don't try to introduce someone to your kids on a first date. Let them know from the beginning that you do have children, but don't impose either on each other. Arrange to meet and say 'Give me time to make sure the kids are settled – don't worry if I'm a few minutes late.' If they stick around they'll soon realize that you and the kids come as a package deal.

What sort of a relationship should you be looking for?

Look for friends rather than romantic partners. One reason for this is that if your separation is fairly recent, you need some time to get over and mourn your loss. Jump straight into a new romance and you don't give yourself time to finish and draw a line under the last relationship.

The other reason is that if you make hunting for a partner your main priority, you may run into trouble. Just as with looking too soon, if you go out with only finding a new squeeze in mind, you may find yourself looking for and falling for someone just like your last partner. You may begin by seeing the same things that drew you to your ex, and end with finding all the faults and drawbacks as well.

There are several advantages to trying to increase the number of friends you have rather than only looking for dates. One is that if you're looking for partners not friends, you may turn your back on anyone who doesn't seem to fit your conditions. So gender, interests or appearance may play a part in your decisions. Which means you may pass up someone with whom you might have had a good friendship and who might have had a sibling or a friend who would have been perfect for you as a date. Another is that friends can often be there for you, strengthening your self-confidence and feelings of self-worth, long after a date has gone on their way.

And if you do meet someone to whom you're attracted, it's always best to begin with friendship before having a romantic relationship. It makes for a far better partnership when it is founded on shared interests or understanding, not just physical attraction.

How to manage your children when looking for a new partner

Starting a relationship on the right foot may be hard if finding a partner is uppermost in your mind. While your feelings and needs may not have changed, your status has. You have children. Which means that anyone you date has to take that in their stride. Inevitably, a single person may feel that even a casual date with someone with children can be awkward. You may just be looking for romance and fun, they may fear you're looking for a partner and a co-parent. And indeed, that may be on your mind too. But with first dates you need to balance a fine line between being honest about your situation as a single parent and not making it part of an expectation. A new person may become someone important in your life and thus to your children, but that is not the way they should begin.

You need to be aware that it may take many dates and much casual fun before you find a new person with whom to share your life. What you, and a potential partner, need to recognize is the pain and confusion your children may feel at the arrival of someone in your life. Your children have either had to process a loss, when a parent left, or have grown up recognizing that their family is them and you and no other. You and they have probably created a tight, close unit in which they rely on you to be there for them. Perhaps they also see their other parent, and have adjusted to knowing that they are there but at a distance. Children in separated families may have to manage feelings of anger, loss and pain; and fears of abandonment and rejection. When a new person comes along, however well they may be managing these feelings, it all may teeter on meltdown. They may fear a new person in your life means that their other parent could be pushed out of their lives forever. Or that you, too, may go away from them, if not in actuality, at least by shifting the bulk of your attention and care to this new person.

How children may react when a new person comes along

Children are not experienced enough to be able to state their feelings clearly. Indeed, they may not even be able to put a name to such emotions. What they are likely to do is to show them, or act them out. As already outlined in Chapter 05, they may react by:

- acting younger than their age
- wetting the bed
- throwing tantrums
- forgetting skills they've learned
- becoming clingy and fretful
- refusing food, being picky or eating too much
- having difficulty sleeping or waking up.

Teenagers may:

- refuse to talk
- be angry
- experiment with drugs, drink, early sex.

When children start acting badly, the first questions you always need to ask yourself are 'What has changed? What has recently happened, or what may they have been reminded of to react this way?' A new person on the scene, a reminder of the fact that their family was once different, can be the trigger for such behaviour. What is underneath their behaviour is often a need for attention, acceptance, and appreciation. They are often fighting to get these needs met when they act up. You can help them by:

- talking openly about the change or loss that has led to their being in a single parent family
- talking about your decision to find new friends
- asking for any questions they may have about this and answering them
- reassuring them that it will not change your feelings for them or your relationship with them
- helping them to show their feelings
- sharing your own feelings with them
- telling them it's okay to feel angry or confused
- asking their opinions
- giving them plenty of time and attention
- making sure some things don't change
- helping them keep in touch with people, places and things that matter to them
- giving them love, reassurance and support
- cutting them some slack and accepting that they will act up.

How to tell your children about new people in your life

Asking their opinions and listening to their feelings is vital. But that isn't the same as asking their permission for you to date or find a new partner, or to let a particular person into your life. That would be shifting the burden onto children in an inappropriate and unfair way. It's also a dangerous tactic. If your child says no, and you accept the veto, what is being said in your family? That adults are no longer in charge or capable of making decisions? That's actually a very frightening prospect for a child. It's one thing to listen with respect and attention to what children feel and need, but another to give them the responsibility of deciding who you can and cannot see.

Sometimes, children may assess what is going on better than their older and 'betters' – an adult may be blinded by love while a child may have realized that the new partner has nobody's interest but their own at heart. But in most circumstances a child will be focusing on their own immediate needs, which in the long run may not do any of the family any good. Sharing information with children and asking for impressions and opinions is an excellent idea. But decisions are for adults and parents to make. That's what being a grown up is all about.

What to say to your children

- When you are ready to date again, you do need to keep your children briefed and well informed. Say to them 'It's time I went out and met new people. I'll be here for you as much as ever and will pay just as much attention to you and spend just as much time with you.'
- When someone does come along, say 'I've met someone I like. We're just seeing each other as friends.'
- If the date works out, say 'I had a really nice time. We're seeing each other again.'
- If this seems the start of something, say 'I'm really enjoying so-and-so's company', and eventually, 'I think this is becoming special.'
- If romance is blooming, say 'Yes, this is definitely becoming special.'
- When the time comes tell them 'So-and-so will be staying over tonight', so nobody gets a surprise in the morning.

- If you do begin to make plans to be together, tell your children straightaway that 'We're talking about moving in with each other', and then, 'We're moving in with each other.'

You will need to reassure them that a new partner for you doesn't mean that your relationship with them changes at all, nor does it change their relationship to their other parent. Children often assume that once a new person moves in, an old one moves out, and they may be afraid that either their relationship with the other parent could be at risk, or indeed theirs with you.

Don't leave them to hear things from other people, or to figure it out for themselves. Secrets can become poisonous and misunderstandings can easily come about. Of course, giving a regular debrief of the progress of a relationship does mean that you have to think about it in clearer terms than you might otherwise have done for yourself. That's one of the issues of being a lone parent; at any other time of your life, things happen and develop and slide by under the radar. When you're in a single parent family, if you want to keep on top of new relationships and deal with the way your children manage them, you need to be analytical and aware.

Being aware of the drawbacks of new dates who are too involved too soon

It's easy to be relieved and pleased when a new date seems not only tolerant but keen to be involved with your children from an early stage. There is a major drawback to this. If someone throws themselves into being a co-parent and then has second thoughts, or if your relationship simply doesn't develop, you won't be the only one disappointed and left with a broken heart. Adults may be able to deal with the sadness of starting and then having to finish a relationship that promised much but did not live up to hopes. Young people who have already lost a family and a parent will find such disappointment much harder to deal with.

Single parents should not be hermits but until they are certain that this relationship is to be serious, the new person in their life is a date, someone to have fun with, to go out with, visit and stay over with and to introduce as a friend but no more. It may be important to hold the boundaries for your children and protect them from feeling that this relationship could be more than it actually is. It does put a tremendous onus on you to find someone who can be positive about them if your relationship does develop, but not jump the gun if it does not, so as not to repeat the loss and pain that the children have already been through.

But taking all that on board, the best message to single parents is 'Go for it'. You deserve new friends and new romance – and you can find them.

Essential points

- You may have to put yourself out there to find a new partner – love seldom comes knocking on your front door without you making some effort.
- Join classes, volunteer, join introduction agencies or internet sites and make sure your friends and family know you're ready to date again.
- Don't feel guilty about attending to what you need. Your children will benefit from you being happy.
- Look for new friends as well as romantic partners. Finding new friends can lead to finding romance.
- Recognize that your children may find a new person in your life difficult to accept. Understand, help and support them but don't be a martyr and give up on what you need.
- Tell your children about a date as soon as possible and keep them briefed as you go along.

Case study

Tasha's ex husband had very little contact with their daughter, Tania, so when she met Wayne and he was not only happy to date her but made a great fuss over Tania, she was delighted. Wayne took Tasha out several times a week and always came over half an hour before they went out so he could read to Tania and play with her. He took them out every Sunday to the park, or to a children's concert, or other event, and after a time Tania started to call him Dad. But after 10 months Tasha began to realize that she and Wayne had less in common than she had thought, and Wayne cooled off. Tasha wasn't entirely surprised or upset when he decided to call it a day, but Tania was devastated. She was furious with her mother and began having major tantrums and rages. She refused to go to bed on time, would get up throughout the night and generally her behaviour worsened. Eventually Tasha asked for advice from her sympathetic GP who helped both of them to recognize and acknowledge how disappointed Tania had been and how understandably let down she had felt. Tania got over her anger but Tasha realized that in future she'd have to pay attention to her daughter's needs and reactions to new partners. She'd have to manage Tania's hopes and not let anyone else, however well-meaning, raise them only to dash them.

Summary

- Dating again can be daunting for you, and upsetting to your children, but that's no reason not to go ahead.
- Any change is hard and you should not be surprised if you find it difficult. Examine the changes in your life calmly and look for the positive side to them.
- You might like to consider all avenues when looking for a new partner. You could try previously unconsidered ones such as dating agencies, marriage bureaus and the internet.
- There is no need to frustrate yourself by trying to be the perfect single parent. The achievable aim, as in any form of parenting, is simply to be Good Enough and to enjoy it and your children.

afterword

A book called Teach Yourself Single Parenting has to highlight the problems since it's all about finding solutions for those problems. So I thought it important to have a final word about the other side. The fact is that single parents do a wonderful job. I hear, and organizations such as One Parent Families with Gingerbread and Parentline Plus hear, from a wide range of lone parents who bring up their children with love and skill and do a very good job of it. These parents and their children don't see themselves as being a problem or part of a problem, or that they are any different from any other family. All families struggle at times, and all families sometimes need a helping hand. Families come in all sorts of shapes and sizes and what really matters is that we do our best to be Good Enough for our children; not perfect, simply Good Enough.

Suzie Hayman, 2008

taking it further

Where to go for help

One Parent Families with Gingerbread provides a helpline with free information to lone parents on issues including benefits, tax, legal rights, family law and contact issues, child maintenance and returning to work. They are able to connect lone parents with other organizations and local groups.
Helpline: 0800 018 5026 (Monday – Friday, 9 a.m.–5 p.m.)
Website: www.oneparentfamilies.org.uk

Parentline Plus is the national charity that works for, and with, parents from families of all shapes and sizes. Parentline Plus provides:
A free confidential, 24-hour helpline: 0808 800 22 22
A free textphone for people with a speech or hearing impairment: 0800 783 6783
Email helpline: parentsupport@parentlineplus.org.uk
Parents Together groups and workshops
Information leaflets
A helpful website: www.parentlineplus.org.uk

MAMA is a UK registered charity which aims to provide friendship and support to all mothers and mothers-to-be, especially those feeling lonely or isolated after the birth of a baby or moving to a new area. By attending a local MAMA group, mums become part of a network of women wanting to make new friends and support each other through good times and bad. This helps alleviate the feelings of isolation and loneliness often experienced by new mothers, which can sometimes lead to, or be part of, postnatal illness.
Helpline: 0845 120 3746 (Monday – Friday, 7 p.m.–10 p.m.)
Website: www.mama.co.uk

SPAN – Single Parent Action Network – is a diverse organization, valuing the vital contributions of one parent families in society.
Telephone: 0117 951 4231
Website: **www.singleparents.org.uk**

Mumsnet offers a supportive community for parents on the web where you can meet mums in your area and further afield, and find out about local activities.
Website: **www.mumsnet.com**

Sure Start is the government programme to deliver the best start in life for every child. They bring together early education, childcare, health and family support.
Telephone: 0870 000 2288
Website: **www.surestart.gov.uk**
For information on Sure Start's Childcare Approval Scheme, call 0845 767 8111 or go to **www.childcareapprovalscheme.co.uk**

Children's Information Services (CIS) hold lists of registered childminders, nurseries and out of school clubs in their areas. Your local Education Department or ChildcareLink (**www.childcarelink.gov.uk**, 0800 096 02 96) can give you the details of your local CIS.

Daycare Trust is the national childcare charity promoting high quality affordable childcare. It publishes *Check Out Childcare*, a guide to choosing childcare.
21 St Georges Rd
Elephant and Castle
London SE1 6ES
Tel: 020 7840 3350
Website: **www.daycaretrust.org.uk**

A **New Deal for Lone Parents** adviser will know about local childcare and can help in making a 'better off' calculation. They can help in looking for opportunities to train or find work. Call the New Deal for Lone Parents Helpline on 0800 868 868 or visit their website: **http://tinyurl.com/354u2a**.

Jobcentre Plus can help with finding training or a job and making benefit claims.
Website: **www.jobcentreplus.gov.uk/JCP/index.html**
You can claim Income Support or Jobseekers Allowance online at **www.dwp.gov.uk/eservice**.

4Children is the national charity that delivers and supports children's centres to extended schools, childcare to play provision, parenting support to support for young people.
Telephone: 020 7512 2100
Website: **www.4children.org.uk**

The Pre-school Learning Alliance is a leading educational charity specializing in the early years, providing practical support to young children and their families.
The Fitzpatrick Building
188 York Way
London
N7 9AD
Email: info@pre-school.org.uk
Website: **www.pre-school.org.uk**

The National Childminding Association can give information on childcare contracts.
Royal Court
81 Tweedy Road
Bromley
Kent BR1 1TG
Tel 0845 880 0044
Website: **www.ncma.org.uk**

Working Families can give information on childcare contracts.
1-3 Berry Street
London
EC1V 0AA
Free helpline: 0800 013 0313
Website: **www.workingfamilies.org.uk**

Home-Start is the UK's leading family support charity offering a range of parenting and family support
Telephone: 0800 068 6368
Website: **www.home-start.org.uk**

Family Welfare Association is a charity offering home and community based support to families in need. They run a network of family centres offering drop in facilities.
501–505 Kingsland Road
London
E8 4AU
Telephone: 020 7254 6251
Website: **www.fwa.org.uk**

CHILD Care Aware is a USA national consumer education parent hotline.
Helpline: 1-800-424-2246
Website: **www.childcareaware.org**

National Child Care Information Center (NCCIC) is a national USA clearinghouse and technical assistance centre that links parents, providers, policy-makers, researchers, and the public to early care and education information.
Helpline 1-800-616-2242
Website: **http://nccic.org**

For information on Child Support in the USA, look for your state child support website at http://**www.acf.hhs.gov/programs/cse/extinf.html** (or **http://tinyurl.com/39jwfj**)

Contact your Child Support Enforcement agency for the forms you need. Agency addresses and telephone numbers are at: **http://ocse.acf.hhs.gov/int/directories/index.cfm?fuseaction=main.extivdlist** (or **http://tinyurl.com/2t4xzc**)

Fathers Direct is the national information centre on fatherhood. They offer publications to support fathers and their families. Their website is at **www.fathersdirect.com**. They also provide a website, **www.dad.info**, which is an online community for fathers with help, advice, forums and features.

Families Need Fathers is a registered charity providing information and support on shared parenting issues arising from family breakdown to divorced and separated parents. Support is provided through a national helpline, a website, a network of volunteers, and regular group meetings, held in a variety of locations.
Helpline: 0870 7607 496 (Monday – Friday, 6 p.m.–10 p.m.)
Website: **www.fnf.org.uk**

Relate offers relationship counselling and life-skills courses through local Relate centres. Counselling is also available over the telephone.
Telephone: 0845 456 1310 (Monday – Friday, 9.30 a.m.–4 p.m.) to find your nearest centre.
Telephone counselling booking line: 0845 1 30 40 16
Website: **www.relate.org.uk**

National Domestic Violence Helpline (run in partnership between Women's Aid and Refuge) provides a free telephone helpline for women experiencing physical, emotional or sexual violence in the home. The free, 24-hour helpline can refer to local refuges and emergency accommodation across the UK.
Helpline: 0808 200 0247
Website: **www.womensaid.org.uk**

National Association of Child Contact Centres promotes safe child contact within a national network of child contact centres. A child contact centre is a safe place where children of separated families can spend time with one or both parents and sometimes other family members. Details of local centres can be found on their website or by ringing them.
Telephone: 0845 4500 280 (Monday – Friday, 9 a.m.–1 p.m.)
Website: **www.naccc.org.uk**

CAFCASS (Children and Family Court Advisory and Support Service) looks after the interests of children and young people involved in cases in the family courts, ensuring their voices are heard. It helps families to reach agreement over arrangements for their children. CAFCASS only works with families on referral from the court but their website contains useful information, case studies, advice and contact links.
Website: **www.cafcass.gov.uk**

Children's Legal Centre offers information on all aspects of child law in England and Wales, particularly contact, parental responsibility and residence orders. A pre-recorded telephone service gives information on frequently asked questions on a wide range of topics. A website and email response service are also available.
Pre-recorded telephone service: 0845 120 3747
Website: **www.childrenslegalcentre.com**

Citizens Advice Bureau is an independent organization providing free, confidential and impartial advice on all subjects to anyone. The address and telephone number of your local CAB can be found in the telephone directory. There is also advice on their website.
Website: **www.citizensadvice.org.uk**
Advice website: **www.adviceguide.org.uk**

Family Rights Group provides a specialist advice and information service for families in England and Wales who are in contact with social services about the care of their children, and their advisers and supporters.
Helpline: 0800 731 1696 (Monday – Friday, 10 a.m.–12 p.m. and 1.30 p.m.–3.30 p.m.)
Website: **www.frg.org.uk**

The **NSPCC** can help with advice on child abuse and keeping your child safe.
Helpline: 0808 800 5000
Website: **www.nspcc.org.uk**

ChildLine (now part of the NSPCC) offers a free confidential helpline open 24 hours.
ChildLine
Freepost NATN1111
London
E1 6BR
Freephone: 0800 1111
Website: **www.childline.org.uk or www.nspcc.org.uk**

It's Not Your Fault is a website for children and young people about divorce and separation, with useful information.
www.itsnotyourfault.org

National Youth Advocacy Service provides advocacy services for children and young people up to the age of 25. They provide specialist help in children's rights, children in care, contact issues, education and youth justice. They have a network of advocates throughout the country and their own legal advice.
Free helpline for children and young people: 0800 616101
Website: **www.nyas.net**
Email advice for children and young people: help@nyas.net

The Site is a website for young people with information about a wide range of local services, as well as discussion forums.
www.thesite.org.uk

Youth Access has a directory of youth advice, information, support and counselling services for young people across the UK. This can be found by ringing their referral line or by looking at the online directory on their website.

Referral information: 020 8772 9900 (Monday – Friday, 9 a.m.–1 p.m. and 2 p.m.–5 p.m.)

Website: **www.youthaccess.org.uk**

Parenting Plans – putting your children first, a guide for separating parents is a very helpful booklet, which acts as an outline for your discussions and agreement. Parent plans help you to think of all the things you will need to manage as parents living apart. It's a booklet of questions that you could use to trigger discussion on issues such as day-to-day arrangements, holidays, health, money, and a section to guide you through what to do if you're finding it hard to agree. You can download this from: **http://tinyurl.com/2c88mz**

Resolution – First For Family Law (the Solicitors Family Law Association) can give advice on any family dispute and with separation, divorce and new families, and encourage mediation and agreement rather than confrontation.

PO Box 302

Orpington

Kent

BR6 8QX

Telephone: 01689 820272

Website: **www.resolution.org.uk**

The Community Legal Service can help you find the right legal information and advice to solve your problems. You can get help through a network of organizations, including:

- Citizens Advice Bureaux
- Law Centres
- independent advice centres
- high street solicitors.

They also provide leaflets on a wide variety of issues to do with separation, divorce and single families.

Telephone: 0845 345 4 345

Website: **www.clsdirect.org.uk**

Family Mediators Association can put you in touch with trained mediators who work with both parents and children.
National Helpline: 0800 200 0033
Website: **www.thefma.co.uk**

National Family Mediation is an umbrella organization for local family mediation services and can provide details of local services in the UK.
Telephone: 0117 904 2825 (Monday – Friday, 9.30 a.m.–3.30 p.m.)
Website: **www.nfm.org.uk**

UK College of Family Mediators can help you to find a mediator.
UK College of Family Mediators
Alexander House
Telephone Avenue
Bristol
BS1 4BS
Telephone: 0117 904 7223
Website: **www.ukcfm.co.uk**

Family Mediation Scotland is at:
www.familymediationscotland.org.uk

Cruse Bereavement Care promotes the well-being of bereaved people and enables anyone bereaved by death to understand their grief and cope with their loss. The organization provides counselling and support, information, advice, education and training services.
Helpline: 0844 477 9400
Young person's helpline: 0808 808 1677
Website: **www.crusebereavementcare.org.uk**

British Association for Counselling and Psychotherapy can recommend a counsellor in your area.
BACP
BACP House
35–37 Albert Street
Rugby
Warwickshire CV21 2SG
Telephone: 0870 443 5219
Website: **www.bacp.co.uk**

The Institute of Family Therapy can help with family problems.
24–32 Stephenson Way
London
NW1 2HX,
Telephone: 020 7391 9150
Website: **www.instituteoffamilytherapy.org.uk**

Separated Dads is a website containing articles and advice for dads living away from their children and offering a regular email newsletter.
Website: **www.separateddads.co.uk**

The Hideout is a site for young people worried about domestic violence.
Website: **www.thehideout.org.uk**

The Advisory Centre for Education (ACE) is an independent, registered charity, which offers information about state education in England and Wales for parents of school age children. They offer free telephone advice on many subjects like exclusion from school, bullying, special educational needs and school admission appeals.

- General advice line: 0808 800 5793 (Monday – Friday, 10 a.m.–5 p.m.)
- Exclusion information line: 020 7704 9822 (24-hour answer phone)
- Exclusion advice line: 0808 800 0327 (Monday – Friday, 10 a.m.–5 p.m.)

Website: **www.ace-ed.org.uk**

Parents Centre is an information and support website for parents on how to help with your child's learning, including advice on choosing a school and finding childcare. It also has online forums for parents to chat to each other.
Website: **www.parentscentre.gov.uk/**

Mind is the leading mental health charity in England and Wales, providing a mental health information service to people by phone, email or letter. They offer support, understanding and information on where to get help, drug treatments, alternative therapies and advocacy.

PO Box 277
Manchester
M60 3XN
Telephone: 0845 766 0163
Email: **info@mind.org.uk**

Young Minds is the charity that is concerned about the importance of children's mental health; the importance of recognizing when a child is troubled and providing adequate support for these children before their problems escalate out of control. They provide a helpline and information for parents and young people.

Helpline 0800 018 2138 (Mondays and Fridays, 10am–1pm; Tuesdays and Thursdays, 1 p.m.–4 p.m.; Wednesdays, 1 p.m.–4 p.m. and 6 p.m.–8 p.m.)

Website: **http://www.youngminds.org.uk/index.php**

Grandparents' Association supports grandparents whose grandchildren are out of contact with them or who have childcare responsibilities for their grandchildren.

Moot House
The Stow
Harlow
Essex
CM20 3AG
Helpline: 0845 4349585
Website: **www.grandparents-association.org.uk/index.asp**

The Child Exploitation and Online Protection (CEOP) Centre works across the UK and abroad to tackle child sex abuse wherever and whenever it happens. Part of their strategy for achieving this is by providing internet safety advice for parents and carers and offering a 'virtual police station' for reporting abuse on the internet.

Website: **www.ceop.gov.uk/index.asp**

Federation of City Farms and Community Gardens can tell you about the farms and gardens open for your children in your area.
The Green House
Hereford Street
Bristol
BS3 4NA
Telephone: 0117 923 1800
Website: **www.farmgarden.org.uk**

UK Parents Lounge has online forums for parents, including a forum specifically for single parents.
Website: **www.ukparentslounge.com**

Parents.com has an online community that includes a Single Mums forum.
Website: **www.parents.com**

Homedads is 'the only UK support group for stay-at-home dads.' It has online forums discussing all the issues of being a dad at home with your kids
Website: **www.homedad.org.uk**

Responsible Single Fathers runs a site for all levels of single fathers including those with residency, with forums. It is an American site.
Website: **http://www.singlefather.org**

The Association of British Introduction Agencies has a list of basic principles and asks members to adhere to their strict code of conduct. You can find a list of members by writing to:
ABIA
Suite 109
315 Chiswick High Road
Chiswick
London
W4 4HH
Telephone: 020 8742 0386
Website: **www.abia.org.uk**

Oh – and if all else fails, my own site: **www.agony-aunt.com**

index

teach yourself

green parenting
lynoa cattanach

- Do you want advice on natural pregnancy and birth?
- Do you want to be an environmentally aware parent?
- Would you like a happy, healthy and balanced family?

Green Parenting is a practical guide to making informed, ethically aware choices for your family. It covers all elements of domestic life, from children and nappies to travel and toys, offering step-by-step advice and useful suggestions for every level of interest and commitment.

Lynoa Cattanach is a director of BabyGROE, a charity promoting a parent-friendly approach to a greener life through its magazines and website.

teach yourself

thrifty living
barty phillips

- Would you like to make your money go further?
- Do you want to know how to cut your bills?
- Would you like to find out how to make money?

Thrifty Living will help you to cut back on your spending and make your money fo further. Whatever your budget, it shows you how to make economies in every area of life, from clothes shopping to cleaning products, with plenty of helpful hints, practical common sence and easy to follow advice.

Barty Phillips is a well-known author, journalist, lecturer and radio and TV broadcaster. She is the author of over 20 books on home and garden subjects, and lectures regularly to a variety of different audiences.